Extension Programme Planning

Extension Programme Planning

Anoop Singh Sandhu
Professor, Extension Education
Punjab Agricultural University
Ludhiana

Oxford & IBH Publishing Co. Pvt. Ltd.
New Delhi
(*A Unit of* **CBS Publishers & Distributors** Pvt Ltd)

CBS Publishers & Distributors Pvt Ltd

New Delhi • Bengaluru • Chennai • Kochi • Kolkata • Lucknow • Mumbai
Hyderabad • Jharkhand • Nagpur • Patna • Pune • Uttarakhand

Extension Programme Planning

ISBN-13: 978-81-204-0911-8
ISBN-10: 81-204-0911-6

Reprint: 2015, 2018, 2022, **2024**

OXFORD & IBH
New Delhi
(A Unit of CBS Publishers & Distributors Pvt Ltd)

Published by **Satish Kumar Jain** and produced by **Varun Jain** for

CBS Publishers & Distributors Pvt Ltd
4819/XI Prahlad Street, 24 Ansari Road, Daryaganj, New Delhi 110 002, India.
Ph: 011-23289259, 23266838 Website: www.cbspd.com
e-mail: delhi@cbspd.com

Corporate Office: 204 FIE, Industrial Area, Patparganj, Delhi 110 092
Ph: 011-4934 4934 Fax: 011-4934 4935
e-mail: publishing@cbspd.com; publicity@cbspd.com

Branches

- **Bengaluru:** Seema House 2975, 17th Cross, KR Road, Banasankari 2nd Stage, Bengaluru 560 070, Karnataka, Ir
  Ph: +91-80-26771678/79 Fax: +91-80-26771680 e-mail: bangalore@cbspd.com
- **Chennai:** 7, Subbaraya Street, Shenoy Nagar, Chennai 600 030, Tamil Nadu, India
  Ph: +91-44-26680620, 26681266 Fax: +91-44-42032115 e-mail: chennai@cbspd.com
- **Kochi:** 42/1325, 1326, Power House Road, Opp KSEB, Power House, Ernakulum Kochi 682 018, Kerala, India
  Ph: +91-484-4059061-65,67 Fax: +91-484-4059065 e-mail: kochi@cbspd.com
- **Kolkata:** 147, Hind Ceramics Compound, 1st Floor, Nilgunj Road, Belghoria, Kolkata 700056, West Bengal, Indic
  Ph: +033-25633055, 033-25633056 e-mail: kolkata@cbspd.com
- **Lucknow:** Basement, Khushnuma Complex, 7 Meerabai Marg (Behind Jawahar Bhawan), Lucknow-226001, U
  Ph: +0522-4000032 e-mail: tiwari.lucknow@cbspd.com
- **Mumbai:** PWD Shed, Gala no 25/26, Ramchandra Bhatt Marg, Next to JJ Hospital Gate no. 2, Opp. Union Bank
  Noorbaug, Mumbai-400009, Maharashtra, India
  Ph: 022-66661880/89 e-mail: mumbai@cbspd.com

Representatives

- Hyderabad 0-9885175004
- Jharkhand 0-9811541605
- Nagpur 0-8692091830
- Patna 0-9334159340
- Pune 0-9664372571
- Uttarakhand 0-9716462459

Printed at Chaman Enterprises, Daryaganj, New Delhi, India

Preface

Extension programmes are the basis of extension teaching and are the means by which the extension service seeks to accomplish its purpose. Results in Extension are dependent on the quality of the programme and the quality is implied by the methods used in developing the programme.

Many questions are raised about the adequacy of the basic theory and methods presently available in the social sciences. That there is a crucial need for developing new theories, improving existing ones and adding additional truths to those now extant is recognised by almost all scientists in extension education.

No one appears to deny that there is a growing body of knowledge in the social sciences that should have application in the real world in which we live and interact. No one can deny that many research workers, professional extension workers and village leaders are concerned about making the greatest possible application of knowledge so that planned change may be as rational and efficient as possible. The extension service through the process of extension programme planning is concerned with how to better apply our present knowledge of human and group behaviour in developing extension programmes that would better serve the needs of the people.

Extension programme planning is a useful, dynamic term when the concepts involved are properly understood and applied. Therein lies the problem of many who are associated with programme planning in extension. Only when the concepts and principles involved are truly understood can methods be devised and techniques developed for their implementation in planning successful ventures involving local people.

The material in this textbook is the result of an effort to bring together the best information available in extension literature.

However, there is still great scope for improving both the selection and the treatment of the subject matter contained herein.

Anoop Singh Sandhu

Punjab Agricultural University
Ludhiana

Contents

1

Extension Programme Planning

To understand the extension programme planning process, certain basic concepts of an extension programme, planning and extension planning need to be understood.

Extension Programme

The word 'programme' has several distinct meanings in the dictionary. It means a proclamation, a prospectus, a list of events, a plan of procedures, a course of action prepared or announced beforehand, a logical sequence of operations to be performed in solving a problem. When used by an organisation, it means a prospectus or a statement issued to promote understanding and interest in an enterprise.

When preceded by the word 'extension', the word takes on several added implications. An extension programme, like that of any other public organisation, should present not only what is to be done, but why it is to be done. It should be an elaboration of the organisation's public policy in such a way that anyone can ascertain just how the programme affects him. In this sense, it is not merely a list of activities or a calendar of work. Some of the definitions of an extension programme given in literature are presented below.

According to Kelsey and Hearne (1949), 'an extension programme is a statement of situation, objectives, problems and solutions'.

Leagans (1961) says that 'an extension programme is a set of clearly defined, consciously conceived objectives or ends, derived from an adequate analysis of the situation, which are to be achieved through extension teaching activity'.

According to the USDA (1956), an extension programme is arrived at co-operatively by the local people and the extension staff and includes a statement of:

i) the situation in which the people are located;
ii) the problems that are a part of the local situation;
iii) the objectives and goals of the local people in relation to these problems; and
iv) the recommendations or solutions to reach these objectives on a long-time basis (may be several years) or on a short-time basis (may be one year or less).

Lawrence (1962) says that 'an extension programme is the sum total of all the activities and undertakings of a county extension services. It includes: (i) programme planning process; (ii) written programme statement; (iii) plan of work; (iv) programme execution; (v) results; and (vi) evaluation.

From the above definitions, it is clear that an extension programme:

— Is a written statement;
— Is the end product of extension programme planning;
— Includes a statement of situation, objectives, problems and solutions;
— Is relatively permanent but requires constant revision;
— May include long-term as well as short-term programme objectives;
— Forms the basis of extension teaching plans;
— Has been drawn up in advance; and
— Has been built on the basis of content.

So, we can define an extension programme as a written statement of situation, objectives, problems and solutions which has been prepared on the basis of an adequate and systematic planning effort and which forms the basis of extension teaching activities in a specific area, for a given period.

Planning

The basic concept of planning appears to be well accepted in our culture. It is regarded as an integral and important dimension of our culture's rational value orientation. Rational value orientation assumes a conscious systematic approach to problem solving, i.e., problem definition, data gathering and choosing between alternative ends and means on the basis of predetermined criteria. Almost everyone accepts the premise that planning is important and necessary for individuals, for families and for business organisations.

According to Myerson and Banfield (1935); 'planning is designing a course of action to achieve ends'.

Efficient planning is that which under given conditions leads to maximisation of the attainment of relevant ends. 'In conceptual thinking, efficient planning refers to reaching decisions through the implementation of a rational planning model' (Myserson and Banfield, 1935). It must be understood that efficient planning is rarely, if ever, achieved in the practical world of plans and planners. So, the most effective planning effort would be that 'which achieves the greatest degree of performance of the actions, motions or operations implied by a set of planning concepts which depict the ideal process' (Boyle, 1965).

Nature of Planning

1. Planning may be a simple process (i.e., planning a lecture) or rather complex (i.e., planning a long-range comprehensive plan for social and economic development of a particular area).

2. Planning is essentially a process of making decisions as to what should be the nature and scope of the objective of the educational agency or organisation. In other words, it may be viewed as preparing a blueprint for action.

3. Without some express purpose, there can be no planning. Planning aims at the optimum use of resources and the rational integration of community life. Within the framework of this broad objective, planning may be done for specialised purposes.

4. Planning is a progressive step-by-step process. It is never completed.

5. Defining of goals is a basic part of planning. In democratic societies, planners do not set these goals alone. Rather they aid the people in defining them. A basic premise underlying this concept is that 'people, when provided with real facts of the situation and with good leadership, will identify the more critical problems with which they are faced' (Peason, 1966). Thus in democratic

planning, both the planners and the people have a distinct and necessary role to play. Therefore, it might be said that one of the prerequisites to democratic planning is awakening of the people.

6. It may be argued that all planning is a social process in the sense that all men are social beings. Thus it might be argued that even a decision regarded as an individual decision in this sense is a social decision as it has been taken on the basis of scientific data as well as personality characteristics. Planning is a social process as it involves some kind of interaction. Interaction assumes some type of communication between two or more people in the planning process. Further, planning is a social process as it affects others. Many individual decisions have their social consequences in terms of interactions with other people, e.g., to inform them, threaten them, reward them etc. On the other hand, when the extension staff as a group, or involving specialists, or by involving key leaders decides on the programme content for the extension education programme for the coming year, it is involved in social planning.

7. Social planning has been defined as a conscious, collaborative, interactional process combining investigation, discussion, agreement and action in order to achieve the conditions, relationship and values regarded as desirable (Beal et al., 1966). This implies planning an action [in order to achieve these conditions, relationships and values regarded as desirable] wherein planning then becomes a means of subjecting social change to value judgements along the intended direction of change and also regarding the appropriate methods to be used to reach these goals. Thus there should be a recognition that individual and societal values are involved in social planning.

Extension Planning

1. Programme planning in extension may now be placed more specifically in this general setting. In no sense is extension unique in these aspects of social planning. All social planning involves these elements, varying only in degree and the specific real world referents. According to Beal et al. (1966), extension is faced with two major problems that dictate that some type of programme planning be done:

i) The great amount of science and technology available in the many disciplines and fields of research;
ii) Limited professional and lay leader resources available to extend this body of science and technology.

2. Extension philosophy strongly stresses the importance of extending scientific and technological know-how that will help members of the various clienteles solve problems that are important to the members of the audience. These facts dictate that some type of priorities be set on the allocation of resources so that optimum aid can be given to the various clienteles. Organising for and determining the programme priorities basically constitutes what is called the programme planning process.

i) First, in the vast majority of cases in extension planning it involves 'a conscious interactional process' involving extension administrators, subject matter specialists, extension supervisors and people's representatives.
ii) Second, it has social consequences as the programme and content areas chosen in the planning process will determine how public funds allocated to extension are used.

3. It should be obvious that values are involved at many stages of programme planning. The fact that a certain method of programme planning is preferred to an alternative method is based on a ranking of values. The fact that certain background information is presented and other background information is not presented, is based on values placed on the criterion selected.

ASSUMPTIONS

The concept of extension planning is based on a number of assumptions. Boyle (1965) has listed the following assumptions in this regard:

1. Planned change is a necessary prerequisite to effective social progress for people and communities.
2. The most desirable change is predetermined and democratically achieved.
3. Extension education programmes, if properly planned and implemented, can make a significant contribution to planned change.
4. It is possible to select, organise and administer a pro-

gramme that will contribute to the social and economic progress of people.

5. People and communities need the guidance, leadership and help of extension educators to solve their problems in a planned and systematic way.

Extension Programme Planning

Having described the concepts of planning and extension programme, now the stage is set to examine the concept of extension programme planning. A few points need to be explicated before attempting a definition.

1. *Extension programme planning is a process:* The dictionary meaning of 'process' is 'any phenomenon which shows a continuous change in time' or 'any continuous operation or treatment'. If we accept this concept of process, we view events and relationships as dynamic, ongoing, ever-changing and continuous. When we label something as a process, we also mean that it does not have a beginning, an end, a fixed sequence of events. It is not static, at rest. The basis for the concept of process is the belief that the structure of physically reality cannot be discovered by man; it must be created by man.

This definition of process suggests that 'a process is involved in which a series of actions culminates in the accomplishment of a goal' (Boyle, 1965). Viewed in this way, the concept of process involves a method, i.e., a process should be viewed as a sequential set of steps or several systematically ordered steps of planning, the performance of which leads to the accomplishment of a goal. In extension programme planning, the immediate goal would be the development of a programme document.

The concept a person has of the extension programme planning process will affect actions and mode of researching the process. Many programme planning processes take place at any particular time at different levels of the extension organisation. For example, programme planning occurs at the national level (five-year plans), at the state level (state plans, annual plans of work) and at the block level. In fact, planning at the block level is taking place when;

i) The long-time plan or projected plan is being developed;
ii) The schematic budget is being planned;

iii) The annual plan of work is being developed;
iv) Detailed plans for individual learning experiences are developed within a major project.

2. *Extension programme planning is a decision-making process:* Planning is basically a decision-making process—and so is extension programme planning. In extension programme planning, scientific facts are put to value judgements of the people through the implementation of a rational planning model in order to decide a programme which will be carried out through the extension teaching activities.

3. *Extension programme planning requires advance thinking:* If we could know 'where we are' and 'where we are to go', we could better judge 'what to do' and 'how to do'. This statement lies at the heart of the nature of planning. Planning does not take place in a vacuum or automatically. It has to be made to happen.

The most basic fact giving rise to planning is that effective rural development results from choice, not from chance; it results from design, not from drift. Good extension programme planning is an intellectual activity since it usually involves a study and use of facts and principles. It requires knowledge, imagination and reasoning ability. It is a complex exercise as it involves people, their needs, their interests, useful technology, educational process, analysing a situation and making decisions about what should be done, determining useful actions, projecting the desired shape of things in future and several other components, which are rarely simple.

4. *Extension programme planning requires skill and ability on the part of planners:* Planning effective extension education programmes requires a number of high-level professional skills. Needed abilities include understanding and skill in the following broad areas:

i) Understanding the nature and role of extension education organisation.
ii) Knowledge and understanding of the technology related to the subject with which the programme is concerned.
iii) Ability to clarify the objectives of a programme and to so state them that they are useful in guiding its execution.
iv) Skill at seeing the relationship between principles and practice.
v) Skill at inquiry and human relationships.

5. *Extension programme planning is built around content:* A programme regarding any extension activity can only be built on the basis of content. Without some express purpose, there can be no planning. Extension programme planning is built around available improved technology, the people, their resources, problems, needs and interests.

6. *Extension programme planning is a social action process:* Extension programme planning involves interaction and the decisions so taken in the form of a programme affect others. Interaction assumes some type of communication between two or more people in the planning process. So when the extension staff involving specialists and people's representatives decides on the programme content for extension teaching for the coming year, it is involved in social planning. In this process, the scientific data is put to value judgements so as to decide the intended direction of change and also the appropriate methods to be used to reach these goals. Further, the resultant programme has many social consequences in terms of interaction with other people, e.g., to inform them, educate them, persuade them, in order to introduce improved technology into their minds and actions.

7. *Extension programme planning is a collaborative effort:* Extension programme planning is a collaborative effort involving identification, assessment, evaluation of needs, problems, resources, priorities and solutions.

8. *Extension programme planning is a system:* Extension programme planning is a system as its procedures and processes are interrelated, ordered and linked progressively to form a collective whole. It includes several subprocesses, such as planning, designing, implementing, evaluation etc.

9. *The end-product of extension programme planning is an extension programme:* The first consideration for anyone who is to concern himself with a process or set of procedures for planning is to clearly identify the primary purpose of the planning process to be developed. Many have suggested that the purpose of planning is for educating those who participate. According to Vandeberg (1965), 'the primary purpose of any planning, first and foremost, is that of developing a sound, defensible and progressive course of action or plan. In the process followed, many other benefits might accrue, such as the education of participants, but we want a plan which can and will be used'.

Extension Programme Planning Defined

Having said that extension programme planning is a social-action, decision-making, interactional process in which advance thinking is needed for identifying the needs, interests and resources of the people through educational means to prepare a blueprint for action, we are now ready to formally define this concept. However, it appears appropriate here to first list some of the definitions of extension programme planning as given in the literature.

1. Programme planning is viewed as a process through which representatives of the people are intensively involved with extension personnel and other professional people in four activities (Boyle, 1965):

—Studying facts and trends;

—Identifying problems and opportunities based on these facts and trends;

—Making decisions about problems and opportunities that should be given priority; and

—Establishing objectives or recommendations for future economic and social development of a community through educational programmes.

2. This is the process whereby the people in the country, through their leaders, plan their extension programme. Country and state professional extension staff members assist in this process. The end-result of this process is a written programme statement (Lawrence, 1962).

3. Extension programme planning is the process of determining, developing and executing programmes. It is a continuous process, whereby farm people, with the guidance and leadership of extension personnel, attempt to determine, analyse and solve local problems. In this, there are three characteristics:

—What needs to be done;

—When it should be done; and

—How it should be done (Musgraw, 1962).

4. An organised and purposeful process, initiated and guided by the agent, to involve a particular group of people in the process of studying their interests, needs and problems, deciding upon and planning education and other actions to change their situation in desired ways and making commitments regarding the

role and responsibilities of the participants (Olson, 1962).

An analysis of these and other definitions of extension programme planning implies that it:

— Is a decision-making, social process;
— Involves advance thinking;
— Is a progressive step-by-step process;
— Involves people in defining the goals to be achieved;
— Uses educational means in defining the goals and situations;
— Is built around improved technology, people, their needs, interests, resources, values, attitudes and skills; and
— The end-product is a written statement of situation, problems, objectives and solutions.

Thus extension programme planning may be defined as:

— A decision-making, social-action process in which extension educationists involve people's representatives,
— To determine their needs, problems, resources and priorities,
— In order to decide on an extension programme consisting of situation analysis, problems, objectives and solutions,
— Which will form the basis of extension teaching plans for a given period.

Rationale of Programme Planning

1. *Progress requires a design:* Effective education is a result of design not drift; it results from a plan—not from trial and error. The experience of workers in extension and in other educational agencies has been that progress is made most effectively when a plan of action is set forth and followed. The pay-off for educational effort comes when people change their behaviour to improve their situation. These results come most rapidly when careful planning is done and when effective teaching methods are used.

2. *Planning gives direction:* There are no tests for directing the people's learning in extension. This augments the difficulty of designing a plan and underscores the fact that planning is one of the most important jobs of extension workers.

In planning or constructing a course of study, the teacher should be guided by five major factors: (1) the purpose for which the course is offered, its aims; (2) the characteristics and needs of those who are to take the course; (3) the educational environment of these persons; (4) the sources of information available; and (5) the requirements or demands of the vocation or other uses to which the learning is to be put. These factors apply to the development of extension programmes as well as to the curriculum of the public schools. The factors that apply to the study of a situation will be considered more closely a little later.

3. *Effective learning requires a plan:* There must be consciously directed effort on the part of the teacher to give guidance to the learning process. The direction of this teaching effort can best be stated in terms of objectives. They must be developed with the people to be taught and must be capable of attainment by and with the people concerned.

Sears (1950) has said that 'planning is getting ready to perform a task'. Time is needed to think through problems, to study situations and to decide upon objectives. Extension workers have been criticised for not having spent sufficient time in planning or for not having given it proper attention. The amount of time devoted to planning, however, must be kept in proper relationship to other tasks. Bryson (1936) states that:

> Men are prone to action....What they need is wisdom before they act....In adult education, there is surely a place for further struggle to slow down man's precipitate and thoughtless speed in action to the end that he may, in the calm interval, attain a clearer definition of his purposes and a clearer vision of the consequences.

4. *Planning precedes action:* The results of an action are dependent on the following: adequacy of analysis of the problems, selection of objectives and involvement of the people. Through the planning process, questions such as these are posed:

i) What information do farm men and women need most?
ii) Which kind of information shall be extended?
iii) What information shall be extended first?
iv) How much time shall be devoted to this line of work?
v) How much effort shall be devoted to this line of work?

The answers to these questions lie in the programme planning process.

Kelsey and Hearne (1949) have given the following rationale

for a planned extension programme. According to them, sound extension programme planning: (i) is based on analysis of the facts in the situation; (ii) selects problems based on needs; (iii) determines objectives and solutions which offer satisfaction; (iv) reflects permanence with flexibility; (v) incorporates balance with emphasis; (vi) envisages a definite plan of work; (vii) is a continuous process; (viii) is a teaching process; (ix) is a co-ordinating process; (x) involves local people and their institutions; and (xi) provides for evaluation of results.

Thus it could be said that planning programmes is an integral part of the development process and ensures better and efficient utilisation of resources, accountability and human development.

2

Principles of Extension Programme Planning

Need for Principles

A principle may be defined as a statement of policy to guide decisions and actions in a consistent manner.

The importance of having certain principles to serve as guidelines in extension programming has been well recognised. Extension education encompasses many phases of farm, home and community life. To develop a programme suited to such vast and varied conditions of human needs and variations is not an easy job. Planning is a complex job and involves a variety of facts, imagination, value judgement, skills etc. So some statements of policy to guide decisions and actions related to programming in a consistent manner are essential in order to develop a plan that will truly reflect the future needs of the extension public.

Sources of Principles

The principles of extension programme planning available in extension literature are based on the philosophy of extension education and on the experience of authors in field extension work. However, most of the statements regarding principles of programme planning have been made by foreign authors (Fanning, 1928; Knans, 1948; Brunner and Yang, 1949; Kelsey and Hearne, 1949; Jans, 1952; Maunder, 1956; Holman, 1957; Randabaugh, 1957; USDA, 1959; Rassi, 1960; Leagans, 1961; Matthews, 1962; Singh, 1962). The original statements of principles of these and other authors are given in Appendix I. A critical look at these principles revealed that they vary in number, sequence, emphasis and sometimes even in spirit from author to author. It is therefore imperative that they be examined for their practicability in the Indian context.

Principles of Programme Planning

After a critical analysis of the programme planning principles available in extension literature, Sandhu (1965) identified a set of principles (Fig. 1) that may be applicable in developing countries. The wording and sequence of these principles have been purposely kept the same as given by Kelsey and Hearne (1949) in so far as possible, in order to maintain uniformity and to avoid further confusion:

Programme

1. Extension programme planning is based on analysis of the facts in the situation.
2. Extension programme planning selects problems based on needs and interests of local people.
3. Extension programme planning determines definite objectives and solutions which offer satisfaction.
4. Extension programme planning has permanence with flexibility.
5. Extension programme planning has balance with emphasis.

Planning Process

6. Extension programme has a definite plan of work.
7. Extension programme planning is an educational process.
8. Extension programme planning is a continuous process.
9. Extension programme planning is a co-ordinating process.
10. Extension programme planning involves local people and their institutions.
11. Extension programme planning provides for evaluation of results.

1. <u>Extension programme planning is based on analysis of the facts in a situation</u>

It is important to take into account the conditions that exist at a particular time. This implies that factors such as land, crops, economic trends, social structure, economic status of the people,

PRINCIPLES OF EXTENSION PROGRAMME PLANNING

PROGRAMME PLANNING PROCESS

EXTENSION PROGRAMME PLANNING

1. IS BASED ON ANALYSIS OF THE FACTS IN THE SITUATION.
2. SELECTS PROBLEMS BASED ON NEEDS AND INTERESTS OF PEOPLE.
3. DETERMINES DEFINITE OBJECTIVES AND SOLUTIONS WHICH OFFER SATISFACTION.
4. HAS PERMANENCE WITH FLEXIBILITY.
5. HAS BALANCE WITH EMPHASIS.
6. HAS A DEFINITE PLAN OF WORK.
7. IS AN EDUCATIONAL PROCESS.
8. IS A CONTINUOUS PROCESS.
9. IS A CO-ORDINATING PROCESS.
10. INVOLVES LOCAL PEOPLE AND THEIR INSTITUTIONS.
11. PROVIDES FOR EVALUATION OF RESULTS.

Fig. 1. Principles of extension programme planning

their habits, traditions and culture, in fact, everything about the area in which the job is to be done and its people, may be considered while planning an extension programme for an area. These factors may be viewed in terms of established long-term objectives and rural policy. The outcome of previous plans should also be reviewed and results utilised.

Brunner and Yang (1949) argue that there is no greater mistake than to assume that technical know-how alone will solve the problems of the farmers. They say that no programme or even technique can achieve the desired results when not in harmony with the culture of the people. 'Extension knows, if need be, the surer way is to effect cultural change by the slow but certain process of education'.

2. Extension programme planning selects problems based on people's interests and needs

Sound programme building selects problems based on people's needs. It is necessary to select these problems which are most urgent and of widest concern. Choice of problems must be from among those highlighted by an analysis of the facts regarding what are felt and unfelt needs. To be effective, extension work must begin with the interests of the families. It must meet interests and use them as a spring-board for developing further interests. It is common knowledge that people join together because of mutual interests and needs.

Brunner (1945) said that an extension programme must meet the felt needs of the people. Leagans (1961) has recommended that the extension workers adopt the subject matter and teaching procedure to the educational level of the people, to their needs and interests, and to their resources.

3. Extension programme planning determines definite objectives and solutions which offer satisfaction

In order to hold interest, we must set working objectives and offer solutions which are within reach and which will give satisfaction on achievement. This is related to motivation for action. People must see how they or their communities are going to benefit from the proposed solutions. Very often the simplicity or dramatic effect of the practice recommended is the most potent factor in its wide adoption. Further, if there is to be progress and not more evolution in the development of man, the objectives must be periodically revised in view of the progress made. In other words, as changes occur, objectives need to be redetermined to allow for even further progress to be realised.

4. Extension programme planning has permanence with flexibility

Any good programme must be forward looking and permanent. Permanence means anticipating years of related and well-organised effort. Along with this lower process, which both follows and makes a long-term trend, experience has shown that particular items will need to be changed to meet unforeseen contingencies or emergencies. Without flexibility, the programme may not, in fact, meet the needs of the people. A programme should be prepared well in advance of its execution but not too far ahead of time. Ordinary events may subject it to change in part though not in total. It is therefore obvious that an extension programme must be kept flexible to meet the changing needs and interests of the people.

5. Extension programme planning has balance with emphasis

A good programme should cover the majority of people's important interests. It must be comprehensive enough to embrace all age groups, creeds and races at all levels and community, block, state, national and international problems. It is futile to deal with only one phase of life in a community as an end in itself. At the same time, a few of the most important or timely problems should be chosen for emphasis. To avoid scattered effort, something must stand out. Decisions must be made as to which of the needs are most urgent. The next consideration in choosing items for emphasis is to promote efficiency by permitting a good distribution of time and effort throughout the year. Too many things carried out simultaneously will divide either the worker's or the people's attention.

6. Extension programme planning has a definite plan of work

No matter how well a programme is thought through, it is of no use unless carried out. This implies good organisation and careful planning for action. A plan of work is an outline of procedure so arranged as to enable efficient execution of the entire programme. It is the answer to what, where, when and how the job will be done. In carrying out programme plans, different leaders and groups may work on various phases, i.e., the women in the community may work on one segment, the men on a second segment and youth-club members on a third. Organisation should be used as a tool to accomplish these purposes, never as an end in itself.

7. Extension programme planning is an educational process

Extension programmes have helped people to solve many problems, but an equally important outcome has been the development of the people themselves to the end that they can more effectively identify and solve the many other problems which confront them. In this aspect, extension planning is unique and differs from planning for highways etc.

In planning extension programmes, acceptance of the importance of need to use intrinsic educational values is an important prerequisite for the development of effective programme procedures. The process of programme planning is in itself an excellent teaching device. This concept should encourage the extension workers to devote sufficient time and effort to developing block extension programmes. People will become interested in the programme when they are involved in the planning process. So, efforts are necessary to involve a large number of people in identifying their needs and significant interests. Effective programme planning is a scientific, problem-solving process, in which skilled thinking is necessary to help people meet and overcome the complex problems of today's society.

The people who do the planning may participate in local surveys and neighbourhood observations. This provides an opportunity for them to learn more about their own community and area and increases their interest. The extension worker has the responsibility of providing local leaders with the knowledge, skills and attitudes they must have if they are to help in educationally serving the people. Essentially, learning takes place through the experiences the learner has and the responses he makes to the stimuli of his environment. The experience gained in finding facts, analysing situations, recognising problems, stating objectives and thinking of possible solutions and alternatives should make for a better and more effective learning environment. The extension personnel should remember this fact and provide opportunities for the effective participation of local people in programme planning.

8. Extension programme planning is a continuous process

Since programme planning is viewed as an educational process and since education is seen as a continuous process, therefore it logically holds that extension programme planning is a continuous process. There is no question of exhausting new knowledge, either in the subject matter with which we deal or in the methods of teaching. With the constant flux of agricultural technology, extension education is faced with an increasingly more difficult job as it tries to serve the needs and interests of the people. Sutton (1961) said that extension in a changing society must adjust and plan for the future to serve the needs of people. He set forth five steps which might be useful in making necessary adjustments:

i) Keep close to the people.
ii) Be flexible and ready to grasp with firmness new problems as they arise.
iii) Work with people in seeking practical solutions to their problems.
iv) Keep abreast of technological and social change.
v) Close the gap between research discovery and practical application.

It is obvious that tomorrow's problem will not be the same as today's. So extension must make periodic adjustments in its plans to meet the changing problems. Extension must also be alert to the change that is going on in science and technology. With new technology, solutions to problems change. It is therefore necessary to view extension programme planning as a continuous process though its recurrence is cyclic.

9. Extension programme planning is a co-ordinating process

Extension programme planning finds the most important problems and seeks agreement on definite objectives. It co-ordinates the efforts of all interested leaders, groups and agencies and considers the use of resources. It obtains the interest and co-operation of many people by showing them why things need to be done. This is important in working with people. Within the extension organisation, the block staff may work together on an integrated programme, each member devoting part of his energy to appropriate phases.

10. Extension programme planning involves local people and their institutions

Involvement of local people and their institutions is very essential for the success of any programme for their development. People become interested and give better support to the programme when they are involved in the planning process. So extension programmes should be planned with the people and not for them.

11. Extension programme planning provides for evaluation of results

Since extension programme planning involves decision-making procedures, so evaluation is important in order to make intelligent decisions aimed at achieving the stated objectives. Matthews (1962) pointed out that extension programme planning and evaluation go together. Kelsey and Hearne (1949) have said that all other principles of programme building are related to evaluation.

Effective evaluation will, of course, depend on clear objectives, knowing which people we are trying to teach and having records of the results in terms that reflect changes in their action. Starting a programme with the intention of engaging in a careful evaluation at the close of a specific period has a salutary effect on all the intermediate processes. However, provision has to be made both for concurrent and ex-*post facto* types of evaluation.

3

A Programme Planning Model

Need for a Model

Good programme planning is primarily an intellectual activity since it usually involves a study and use of facts, skill and principles. It requires knowledge, imagination and reasoning ability. Often it requires a mastery over special skills and techniques tested by empirical evidence. It is basically a process of making decisions that will be carried out in future.

Sound extension programmes are planned with the people and not for them. Participation of the local people with extension workers in studying and analysing the situation, in singling out problems, fixing priorities and giving them design, has been recognised the world over. This also enables the extension agency to realise the limits of people's capabilities and possible contribution to the implementation of programmes. With the introduction of the three-tier Panchayat Raj system in India, people have been entrusted with the opportunity of tailoring the programmes themselves with the extension agency providing expert guidance.

These factors and other principles of programme determination are of no value unless adopted and applied to a large extent. But to develop an extension programme suited to the vast and varied nature of extension work is no easy job. Since it involves several complex problems, a workable procedure needs to be formulated and well understood. Although procedures for extension programme planning have to be provided with ample latitude for adjustment needed to meet local situations, yet they have to be adequately definite to be able to give general direction.

Evolution of the Model

According to Vandeberg (1967), planning properly done is an investment of time that should pay high dividends. It is a positive, dynamic, useful and effective term when the concepts involved are understood and applied. Various philosophers, theorists and educators in the field of extension education have suggested from time to time a number of useful models for planning an extension programme.

After a critical analysis of over 20 such models available in the literature throughout the world (some are presented in Appendix II) and keeping in view the Indian conditions, Sandhu (1965) developed a model for planning extension and rural development programmes. This model has six phases with a number of steps to be followed under each phase (Fig. 2). The various phases and steps involved in this model are:

I. Organisation for Planning

II. Planning Process:

1. Reach understanding regarding principles, procedures, roles and time schedule.
2. Analyse situation.
3. Determine objectives.
4. Select problems with due regard to priorities.
5. Find solutions.

III. Planned Programme:

Prepare a written statement of:

i) situation;
ii) objectives;
iii) problems; and
iv) solutions.

IV. Plan of Work:

Prepare a plan of work containing information regarding:

i) people to be reached;
ii) goals, dates and places;
iii) teaching procedures to be followed;
iv) duties, training and recognition of leaders;
v) roles to be played by extension personnel; and
vi) roles to be played by other agencies.

V. Execution of plan of work:

i) Make advance arrangement for inputs and teaching aids.

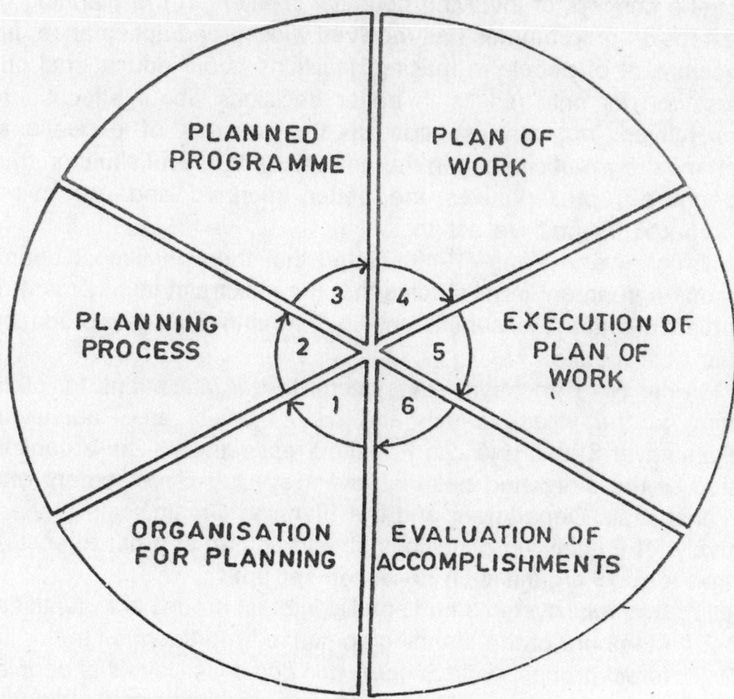

PLANNING PROCESS INVOLVES

1. REACHING UNDERSTANDING REGARDING PRINCIPLES, PROCEDURES, ROLES AND TIME SCHEDULE.
2. ANALYSING SITUATION
3. DETERMINING PROGRAMME OBJECTIVES
4. SELECTING PROBLEMS
5. FINDING SOLUTIONS

Fig. 2. Extension Programme Planning Model

ii) Interpret the approved programme to the staff and people's representatives.

iii) Carry out the planned programme, phase by phase, in a co-ordinated manner.

VI. Evaluation of accomplishment:

i) Do concurrent evaluation.

ii) Do ex-*post facto* evaluation.

ORGANISATION FOR PLANNING

The concept of involving potential clientele in the planning of extension programmes has received widespread acceptance. Involvement of people in making decisions about educational objectives not only results in better decisions about educational objectives, but also speeds up the process of educational change. By participating in the analysis of the local situation, the people's representatives are better informed and are better prepared for positive action.

Brunner and Yang (1949) stated that there is almost unanimous agreement in all studies that the maximum involvement of potential and actual constituents in programme building produces the best results.

Under the Panchayat Raj system, the organisations for planning at the village, block and district levels are Panchayat, Panchayat Samiti and Zila Parishad respectively. The organisation at the state and national levels are the Development and Panchayats Department and the Planning Commission respectively. The following conditions should be met in order to ensure that a good organisation has been set up:

1. All social systems and special interest groups are identified.
2. Members of the planning committee represent all major interest groups, various economic and social levels of people, major vocations of the locality and other important elements in the area.
3. Each member of the planning committee clearly understands—
   a) the purpose of the group;
   b) how the group should function in attaining its purpose; and
   c) his individual role as a member.
4. Members of the planning committee have been elected, nominated or co-opted by appropriate democratic procedures.
5. Each member has a designated period of time to serve on the committee.
6. There is a specific date and procedure for replacement of each member to ensure continuity of the programme planning committee.

PLANNING PROCESS

1. <u>Reaching understanding regarding principles, procedures, roles and time schedule</u>

It is necessary that all staff and the people's representatives be familiar with the principles and procedures of programme planning for the purposes of clarity and uniformity of action. It is necessary to hold a meeting to discuss the principles to be kept in view, steps to be followed, roles to be performed and the time to be followed. The following conditions should be met in order to fulfil the spirit of this step:

i) A clearly defined statement of purpose is given by the planning committee.
ii) The statement of purpose is accepted by:
   a) extension staff;
   b) planning committee members; and
   c) other professional leaders working with the committee.
iii) Uniform understanding of the purpose of the committee on the part of individual members.
iv) Clearly defined written statements of:
   a) the role of the extension workers in programme planning;
   b) the role of the planning committee members and other professional leaders;
   c) the purpose of programme planning;
   d) the scope of extension's educational responsibilities;
   e) the procedures to be followed;
   f) the principles to be kept in view; and
   g) the procedures to be followed.
v) The block, district and state level extension workers and programme planning committee members have understood:
   a) the role of extension workers in programme planning
   b) the role of programme planning committee members;
   c) the purpose of programme planning;
   d) the scope of extension's educational responsibilities;
   e) the procedures to be followed;
   f) the principles to be kept in view; and
   g) the time schedule to be followed.

2. Analyse situation

Situation analysis involves collection, analysis and interpretation of the existing facts. Good planning depends on the availability of adequate and reliable data and scientific elaboration and interpretation of the same. Extension workers must have adequate knowledge of what farmers produce and how the production can be stepped up to the maximum.

An intimate knowledge of the cropping patterns, procedures of farm management and factors of production is essential for purposeful programme planning in agriculture. Hence it is of great importance that all extension workers possess the factual and basic farm and family information for preparing sound family, village and block plans. There is no research evidence, however, to suggest what kind and type of specific information ought to be collected and used for this purpose.

The data collected should be analysed and evaluated with the help of the entire team of extension workers and with the active participation of people's representatives. The following criteria should be met in order to ensure that this step has been adequately followed:

i) Facts needed to evaluate the accomplishment of the previous year's programme are collected.
ii) Pertinent state, national and international basic facts are assembled and made available to the planning committee for their use in identifying problems.
iii) Pertinent state, national and international facts are assembled by:
    a) extension staff; and
    b) appropriate state extension specialists.
iv) Local facts needed to define correct and projected needs and interests and problems of the area are assembled.
v) Needed facts are collected by:
    a) concerned extension staff;
    b) committee and subcommittee members;
    c) appropriate state extension specialists; and
    d) other local people.
vi) The basic facts assembled and collected about background information are analysed and interpreted.
vii) The situation revealed by the interpretation is projected.

viii) The following groups are involved in the interpretation and projection of the basic facts:
   a) Area extension staff
   b) Planning Committee members
   c) Appropriate State Extension Specialists
   d) Other local people

ix) The major needs and problems of the area which are within the scope of extension's educational responsibility are identified.

x) The following groups are involved in identifying the major needs and problems of the block:
   a) Area extension staff
   b) Planning Committees
   c) Appropriate State Extension Specialists
   d) Other resource persons
   e) Other local people

3. <u>Determine objectives</u>

It is essential in the programme planning process that before deciding on the projects to be undertaken, basic objectives of the programme are determined by the villagers in consultation with the extension staff. The objectives should be determined on the basis of the situation analysis. Determination of objectives is the most important function of extension programme planning. The following conditions or qualities will exist when objectives have been determined adequately and properly:

i) Objectives have been determined relative to major problems, need and/or interests as determined by the programme planning committee.

ii) Both immediate and long-term objectives have been determined.

iii) The following people have been involved in the determination and acceptance of objectives:
   a) Members of the programme planning committee.
   b) Members of the panchayat institutions.
   c) Area extension staff
   d) District level specialists
   e) Other resource persons
   f) Other local people, both elected and nominated.

4. Select problems with due regard to priorities

Selection of problems to be tackled will involve identification, classification and selection with due regard to priorities. Identification of problems will be done on the basis of situation analysis. Once the problems have been identified, it is desirable that they be properly classified into the following categories:

a) Problems which can be solved by the people themselves with no outside financial aid.

b) Problems which can be solved by the people with the aid of the Panchayat Samiti.

c) Problems which can only be solved with the help of Government funds.

In view of the limited resources and unlimited problems, it is essential that some problems which need immediate solution should be selected for formulating programmes to solve them. Trying to meet all needs at any one time may be beyond the planners. It may confuse the villagers and is certainly unnecessary. Efforts should be made to select problems, therefore, with due regard to priorities both form the point of view of the national needs and people's interests. In other words, it is necessary for the extension planners and the people's representatives to select problems and fix priorities based on their needs and the resources and technology available.

The following conditions will exist when the requirements of this step have been adequately met:

i) All the problems that can be solved by the villagers with their own resources have been determined.

ii) Problems that can be solved by the Panchayat Samiti with its own resources are determined.

iii) Those problems that can only be solved by Government funds are also determined.

iv) All the problems in the areas are collected and identified democratically through participation of village people, the entire extension staff and others who contribute to the programme.

v) Of the identified problems, the most felt and of widest concern are selected by the extension agents and people's representatives.

vi) Selected problems are related to the family, community,

block and district situation.

vii) For tackling the selected problems, the time is scheduled on greatest priority basis.

viii) Priorities are determined relative to the major problems, needs and interests as determined by the planning committee.

ix) The extension workers and the programme planning committee members are involved in determining priorities.

5. Find solutions to problems

The Village Level Workers at the village level and the Agricultural Extension Officer at the block level are two most important functionaries who advise the village families and the village institutions regarding solutions to their problems. The Assistant Extension Specialists and the District Agricultural Officer can join the block team to help the people and the Panchayat Samiti in finding solutions to agricultural problems of the area. Experiences of the farmers and suggestions of the specialists will help in arriving at a joint decision.

The following conditions will exist when this step has been properly carried out:

i) All the available research findings in the State are collected and projected.

ii) Suitable solution to the problems according to the research findings are made by block level and district level specialists.

Planned Programme

It has been said that an extension programme is a written statement of situation, objectives, problems and solutions which has been prepared on the basis of an adequate and systematic planning effort and which forms the basis of extension teaching plans.

As Leagans (1961) pointed out, it is of utmost importance that the staff and the people in each area not only develop an extension programme, but also prepare the programme in a written form that is readily understood and is suitable for obtaining approval and use as a guide for officials and non-officials.

The problems should be stated from the viewpoint of the farm, the home and the community. They should not be stated in terms of solutions. The objectives should also be stated at a lower level in specific and measurable terms. They should include details about the learners to be reached, subject matter to be taught and the behavioural changes to be effected. The objectives may also be stated from the point of view of the extension organisations and the extension puhlic.

Although the solutions, recommendations or teaching will vary with different situations and although there are many exceptions, it is essential to be concise and clear in stating solutions to the problems. Extension workers should not offer to help the extension public with problems for which no adequate or practical solution is available.

The following conditions will be met in order to have a good programme statement:

i) The written programme should be suitable for use by the staff, planning groups and other individuals or groups concerned with the programme.
ii) It should state the primary facts that clearly reveal the situation for major subject or problem areas.
iii) It should clearly state the important problems or needs identified by the staff and the people in the programming process.
iv) It should state both the long-term and short-term objectives for each major subject or problem area that is to be focussed on in programme execution over a period of time.
v) It should state the objectives of the programme in a form that—
   a) clearly reveals the kind of new condition or situation desired;
   b) is meaningful to the staff and the people; and
   c) will serve as a useful guide to programme execution.
vi) It should specify the subject matter related to each objective that is highly significant to the people, socially or economically or both.
vii) It should include a summary of the long-term programme prepared in a form suitable for public distribution, containing the following items:
   a) It should be made available in a summary form containing major facts about the overall area situation.

b) Brief statements of the organisation and its objectives and philosophy.

c) Brief descriptions of the situation, statements of major problems, long-term objectives and major means of achieving them for each of the major subject or problem areas.

d) The names of members of the planning groups and the official staff.

e) Other appropriate information.

viii) It should be made available in a summary form to all the members of the planning groups and the professional staff.

ix) It should be circulated by appropriate means so that the general public can understand its nature and objectives.

x) It should be used as the basis for developing annual plans of work.

Plan of Work

Preparing a plan of activities directed towards solving selected problems is an important step. A plan of work is the listing of activities by which the objectives already decided upon are to be achieved. It includes the methods of carrying out the programmes such as demonstrations, meetings, farm contacts by the extension workers etc. It indicates the places, times and persons responsible for carrying out the programme as well as the method of evaluating progress. Thus it answers the questions of what, how, when, where and by whom the work is to be done. A well-prepared plan of work will provide details about:

i) people to be reached;
ii) goals, dates and places;
iii) teaching procedure to be followed;
iv) duties, training and recognition of leaders;
v) part to be played by extension personnel;
vi) part to be played by other agencies.

The following conditions should exist in a good plan:

i) The plan of work is in written form.
ii) It has been developed co-operatively by the extension workers and samiti members.
iii) It identifies the specific educational job to be done.
iv) The specific educational jobs are related to general objec-

tives in the programme as planned.

v) The plan indicates for each educational job:
   a) How it will be done
   b) When it will be done
   c) Where it will be done
   d) Who will do it
   e) What people are to be reached

vi) The plan of work includes a calendar of activities and events.

vii) The people who are to do each of the educational jobs as outlined in the plan participate in developing the plan and accept their respective responsibility.

viii) Techniques, methods and materials and other resources are indicated for each major problem and are appropriate for the objectives to be accomplished.

ix) Identification of subjects matter to be covered is included for the educational jobs to be done.

x) The subject matter is appropriate considering the people's level of interests, knowledge, attitude and available time and technology.

xi) The plan provides for the needed training of extension workers and leaders.

xii) Specific changes to be achieved or evidence of accomplishment are indicated clearly.

Implementation Phase

1. Make advance arrangement for inputs and teaching aids

After the plan of work is ready, it is necessary to make advance arrangements for the supplies needed, such as seeds, fertilisers, insecticides-pesticides, credit facilities etc. Similarly, teaching aids, such as audio-visuals, literature, exhibits etc. should also be prepared and procured in sufficient quantity and well in time.

The conditions to meet the requirements of this step are:

i) Realistic needs of inputs such as fertilisor, seeds, credit facilities etc. have been worked out jointly by the area extension staff and the Panchayat Raj institutions.

ii) Needed inputs have been procured well in time and stocked at proper places.

iii) Teaching aids to be used by the extension workers have been prepared and/or procured in sufficient quantity, well in time.

2. Interpret the approved programme to the staff and the samiti members

Although the extension programme has been planned with the active participation of extension workers and the Panchayat Samiti members, stills there is need that the approved programme be interpreted to the extension staff and the people's representatives. First, all the extension staff and samiti members may not have been involved in planning. Secondly, some changes may have been made by the programme sanctioning authorities.

The following criteria will be met to ensure that this step has been adequately undertaken:

i) The approved programme has been explained adequately.
ii) The plan of work has also been explained adequately.
iii) They have been explained to all the block staff, all the samiti members and other important leaders.

3. Carry out the plan of work

The approved programme should be carried out, step by step, according to the plan of work and in a co-ordinated manner. The success of a programme depends on the methods used to implement it. There is no single extension teaching method that may be good under all conditions. Further, a proper combination of extension teaching methods is a must. Research evidence shows that there is need for a planned communication strategy for effective implementation of a programme. It should be ensured that—

i) The plans for co-ordination within extension were followed as planned after periodic evaluation indicated that no changes were required.
ii) The plans for co-ordination outside extension were followed as planned after periodic evaluation indicated that no changes were required.
iii) Changes in the plans for co-ordination within extension were made after re-evaluation replanning and decisions and were followed as planned.

iv) Changes in the plans for co-ordination outside extension were made after re-evaluation, replanning and decisions and were followed as planned.

v) Decisions for changes in the plan of work for co-ordination were made by the agents concerned, representatives from the planning groups and representatives from the groups concerned or involved.

vi) The calendar of activities and events was followed as planned after periodic re-evaluation which indicated no changes were required.

vii) Changes in the calendar were made after re-evaluation, replanning and decisions and were followed.

viii) Decisions for change in the calendar were made by the agents concerned and representatives from planning groups and other groups and state staff who were involved.

ix) Techniques, methods and materials used were varied and appropriate to the situation.

x) Planned techniques, methods and materials were re-evaluated periodically and used as planned or as replanned.

xi) The subject matter was used as planned after periodic re-evaluation and decision that no changes were necessary.

xii) Changes in subject matter were made and justified on the basis of re-evaluation, replanning and decisions.

xiii) Decisions for changes in subject matter were made and approved by the agents involved after consultation with the appropriate subject matter specialist, supervisors and representatives of planning groups.

xiv) The subject matter used was appropriate, considering the people and their objectives.

xv) The plans for shared responsibilities were followed as planned after periodic re-evaluation which indicated changes were not necessary.

xvi) Changes in the plans for shared responsibilities were made and followed after re-evaluation, replanning and decisions.

xvii) Decisions for change in the plans for shared responsibilities were made and effected by the agents concerned and all other individuals involved.

Evaluation of Accomplishments

Concurrent and ex-*post facto* review of progress towards the objectives is an essential phase of extension programme planning. This keeps the extension agency on the right track and helps in differentiating means from ends. Evaluation of the activities should be undertaken jointly by the extension staff and the people's representatives organisations at different levels. Most programme organisations make a provision for fortnightly, quarterly and annual evaluation of programmes. Planning of future programme should be based on the evaluation results of the previous one. Successful evaluation gives a correct direction and speed to a programme. Conditions that will exist when this guideline is met are as under:

i) Evaluation plans were developed for each of the phases of the programme to be evaluated as indicated in the annual plan of work.
ii) Evaluations of accomplishment were based on data from adequate samples.
iii) Data for evaluation of accomplishment was collected through the use of appropriate techniques and devices.
iv) Findings were based on adequate facts which had been carefully analysed and interpreted.
v) Findings were translated into programme implications for use in programme executes.
vi) Materials were developed for the specific purpose of reporting accomplishments.
vii) A variety of channels or media were used in reporting and interpreting accomplishments to the general public.
viii) A report of accomplishments and implications was made to the extension governing group. The findings from the report of accomplishments and implications were given careful consideration by the governing group in projecting their plans for extension in the county.
ix) A report of accomplishments and implications was made to the programme committee.
x) Findings from the report of accomplishments and implications were studied by the Planning Committee and used in developing the county extension programme.

4

Situation Analysis

Situation analysis is one of the most important steps in the programme planning process. It involves collection, compilation and analysis of facts in a given situation in order to identify local needs, interests, problems and priorities. In order to analyse a situation properly and effectively, it may be necessary to understand the concept of people's needs and interests. As Leagan (1961) has said, sound extension programmes are based on people's needs and interests to make them significant and effective. People's participation in programme implementation is likely to be greater if a programme reflects their needs and interests.

Concept of Needs

Every person is continuously striving to fulfil his needs and to find conditions wherein he can maintain satisfaction for the fulfilment of his needs. They may be classified into three categories: (1) those of a physical nature; (2) those of a social nature, indicating such things as social status or the feeling of belonging; and (3) those of an integrative nature, such as philosophy and religion.

A need is the lack of something that, if present, may further the welfare of an individual. Anything that is requisite to the maintenance of a state of affairs is a need. Hence a need is the difference that exists between the actual situation and what the situation ought to be. The nature and extent of need (width of gap) is an indication of significance of the problem.

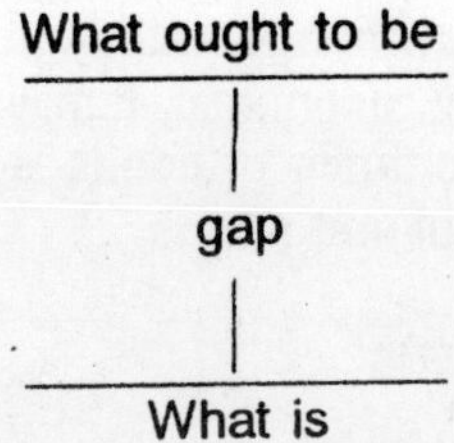

People must be brought to recognise the gap between the actual or what is and the desirable, or what ought to be, and to place a value on attaining the desirable condition before they will want to change or become motivated to change in progressive directions. The educational process brings people to recognise the differences in these situations and to determine their needs, which may be classified as: (1) felt or recognised and (2) unfelt or unrecognised. The current behaviour of people is largely determined by their felt needs. Motivation comes with a felt need. The job of the educator is to help an individual recognise an unfelt need and also the obstacles to achieving his goal.

Characteristics of Needs

Some primary characteristics of needs are:

1. All people have needs; not to have them would constitute utopia.
2. Needs represents a gap between the status quo and what should be or between what is and what ought to be.
3. People have to recognise the difference between the actual and the desirable and place a value on attaining the desirable before they become motivated to change.
4. The width of gap is indicative of the extent of the need.
5. Needs can commonly be grouped into three categories.
   (a) Physical
   (b) Social
   (c) Integrative
6. Needs can be psychologically classified into two group:
   (a) Felt
   (b) Unfelt
7. Needs tend to be individual in nature, but also tend to be common to members of groups.
8. Needs change with time and progress.

9. Needs of people change with age and growth and with changes in social, economic, family status etc.
10. The relative importance of needs is influenced by physical conditions and cultural norms.

Determination of Needs

It has been said that needs imply a gap between what is and what ought to be. Needs are identified by finding through the planning process the actual, the possible and the valuable.

— What is can be determined by a study of the situation.

— What ought to be can be determined by research findings and the values people hold.

— Information about what is does not make a programme, it only shows the situation. From this point planners have to take another step and decide what ought to be.

— Deciding on what ought to be is the process of deciding on programme targets, goals or objectives.

— The level of what ought to be must be within the physical, economic, social and mental possibilities of attainment.

Interests

The extension worker needs to be alert to the interests of the people for it is largely through one's interests that a person's accomplishments in life are determined. As a rule people learn those things that lead towards the attainment of their goals or their wants. For this reason, a knowledge of interests is important to the educator. What a person wants has an influence upon his learning. If interest in an existing need is not present, it is the job of the extension educator to create such interest.

The following may be said of interests:

1. People who are interested in certain problems or needs will acquire more information about them.
2. People tend to expose themselves to information which is congenial to the interests they already hold.
3. Interests usually represent the objectives of the individual.
4. Interest is the most important phase of motivation.
5. Interest gives the learner satisfaction when met.
6. Present interests provide a starting point in the learning process.

7. Interest tends to control the distribution of extension education.

These statements serve as useful criteria to the Extension Worker in guiding people in the process of programme building.

Effective programme building is dependent on accurate determination of the needs and interest of people. Extension Workers need to have an understanding of the nature of needs and interests to develop more effective programmes.

Situation Analysis

As stated earlier, an effective situation analysis will involve collection of relevant facts in the situation, their compilation and analysis.

Collection of Relevant Facts

Human element: In extension programme planning, an accurate determination of a situation is dependent on data that includes several kinds of information. The people themselves are the first important source of information. From them can be obtained their:

i) Interests;
ii) Opinions regarding needs;
iii) Attitudes;
iv) Knowledge of conditions affecting the problem;
v) Possible solutions;
vi) Actual practices; and
vii) Their goals.

The important thing to remember in collecting data is that it must be pertinent to the problem at hand and also must be valid.

Physical situation: The physical situation provides the second source of information regarding economic and social factors affecting the problems under consideration. Knowledge of the physical situation should include information about:

i) Land;
ii) Crops;
iii) Livestock;
iv) Type and size of farms;
v) Farm and home practices being followed;

vi) Community facilities etc.

Public policy: Public policy affords the third source of information regarding a situation. The public policy of any organisation may dictate the limitations of the solution to a problem. Extension education incorporates policies that affect and protect its educational programmes. Other organisations may have policies that affect groups of people and consequently may limit or help to define the solution to a problem. A consideration of the National and State policies will help in giving direction to the planning process.

Extension agency: Professional extension workers provide the fourth source of information. The extension workers of a block need to help the people think through the kinds of information needed and to determine the means of selecting data in certain instances. Their responsibility is to obtain the combined reactions.

The extension worker can supplement the data obtained from the people by recognising their unfelt needs and by recognising the relationship between problems that lay people might overlook. The supervisors assist in giving extension workers direction in the overall planning process. Supervisors may be helpful in providing information regarding the general situation in a block and in relating local problems to state and national problems. The specialist's main contribution is that of 'what should be'. Specialists are a source of technical information for solving certain problems. They can draw upon scientific research, their own study and experience in working with people to aid in the solution of problems.

In determining the situation from the above four sources of information, the answers to the following kinds of questions must be determined:

1. How many people for whom the improved practice is appropriate are actually following it?
2. Who are the people, following/not following the practice?
3. Why are some people not following the improved practice?

Analysis of facts: The collection of data is but a means to an end. Facts per se do not make a programme; they only show what the situation is. The collection of data is useful only to the extent that it helps to further identify the needs and interests of people and aids in finding solutions to problems. Extension workers need to guide the collection of data. The planning process can become 'bogged down' with facts resulting in lay people becoming discouraged because they cannot see the relevant value of the facts. A whole roomful of facts may be gathered but only a handful of them may be useful in defining the problem.

Once needs and problems have been recognised, the question remains as to the number and kinds of objectives that can be worked upon effectively. The important thing is not who makes the decision about what shall be undertaken, but rather what was the basis for making the decision. The selection of objectives may be determined by a pooling of judgements in terms of:

i) Significance of people's needs and interests.
ii) Social and economic importance of a given need to the people.
iii) Relative significance of one objective in view of another.
iv) Significance of working on the objective immediately.

Let it be emphasised once again that an adequate analysis of a situation forms the basis for deciding what will receive attention in a given period. The solution to a problem can be no better than the facts upon which it is based.

Rapid Rural Appraisal

Amongst the various approaches used in situation analysis, rapid rural appraisal—an interdisciplinary approach for assessing local people's needs—is becoming very common.

Rapid rural appraisal (RRA) is a quick approach to analysing a situation for assessing farmers' needs by a multidisciplinary team through a creative and structural use of investigation tools in a more accurate and cost-effective manner.

This technique was developed initially by social scientists to allow planners to obtain timely information about the sociocultural dimension of natural resource management problems. It has now become a multidisciplinary approach for securing and analysing information on a variety of technical subjects. This approach is being used by an increasing number of technical specialists and project staff for assessing information on important aspects and client needs.

The quality of the results depends heavily on the team's ability to make analytical judgements on picking up key issues within a short period of time. According to Molner (1989), when properly used, RRA tools can generate reliable and substantial information about problems of natural resource management.

Characteristics

Some of the salient characteristics of this technique are:

i) *Rapid:* It is rapid as the results are made available to the decision makers in a short time.

ii) *Eclectic:* It allows picking up investigation tools that enable tailoring interview and survey techniques to meet the needs of specific information gathering.

iii) *Holistic:* Its use makes it possible to capture a multidisciplinary picture of a local situation.

iv) *Interactive:* It allows adequate interaction between researchers and project clients.

v) *Interdisciplinary:* It is interdisciplinary and includes decision makers, researchers, social scientists as well as extension workers, women and key informants to dialogue issues.

vi) *Cost-effective:* It provides reliable and sufficient information in a relatively shorter and more flexible time frame.

vii) *Shared perspective:* It changes the perspective of technical experts regarding their own topics and helps them redefine their judgements from a shared perspective.

viii) *More realistic:* This technique is midway between formal and non-structured methods of situation analysis and hence is a more realistic approach for a short time frame.

RRA Tool Kit

The RRA tool kit includes:

1. Questions and interview design techniques for individuals, households, groups and key informants.
2. Sampling techniques that can be adopted to a particular objective.
3. Methods of obtaining quantitative data in a short time frame.
4. Methods of direct observations at site.
5. Group interview techniques including focus-group interviewing.

6. Methods of cross-checking information from different sources.
7. Use of secondary data sources.

The choice of various investigations tools will depend on the time available, constitution of the team, nature of secondary data available, complexity of the situations to be analysed etc.

Interdisciplinary Team Interaction

The team will consist of a subject matter specialist, a social scientist, an extension worker, an expert on woman and a guide or interpreter. The role of the extension and social scientists in the team is:

i) to collect relevant socioeconomic information;
ii) to introduce a social perspective to team members; and
iii) to provide training in methods of interviewing.

Team members meet regularly to redefine objectives, discuss emerging hypotheses and to reallocate time and resources.

Team members split into pairs each day of field visits during the period of information collection, so that members of different disciplines benefit from interacting with each other on a one-to-one basis. However, splitting team members for daily field visits will also depend on logistics, e.g., vehicles available, road network, distance involved etc.

Sampling Methods

Selection of respondents for interviewing is one of the most crucial issues in the RRA. Opinions vary widely on this subject. Some authors prefer purposive, others a randomised sampling. Perhaps, a stratified sample would be a better alternative. Furthermore, indepth and open-ended interviews are likely to reduce the non-sampling errors.

Preselection of zones with different characteristics may be useful. Respondents to be selected should include individuals, groups, households, women and key informants.

When households are reluctant to give accurate information on sensitive issues, direct measurements, secondary data and casual conversations may have to be used.

Question Design Techniques

Acquiring expertise in designing questions for sensitive and non-biased interviewing is a slow process requiring training and field experience. However, in designing questions for individuals or households, the following points may be kept in view:

1. Avoid questions that are so phrased as to lead the respondents to a particular answer.
2. Use six helpers (what, where, who, when, how and why) to ensure that the interviewer understands the situation rather than draws conclusions from partial information.
3. Probe questions.
4. Use local names.
5. Elicit local system of classification. These things are relevant to the project.
6. Collect information about the history of resource use.

For an intrahousehold perspective never assume that one member of the household can speak for all the rest. Women have different knowledge and opinions than do men. They are also less accustomed to formal interviews and hence questions should be short, simple and straightforward.

Key informants (persons with special knowledge of a given topic) are a major source of information for interviews bound by a time constraint. They can be used for soliciting specific information as well as in evaluating another person's opinions.

Interview techniques include:

1. Do not disrupt the respondent's normal work routine.
2. Order questions properly.
3. Include more open-ended questions.
4. Allow members to express themselves freely.
5. Women speak more freely inside their houses.
6. Interview leaders first to legitimise.
7. Subdivide groups, if large.
8. Vary topics to hold interest.
9. Include humour when pointing out any shortcoming.
10. If people are reluctant to give accurate information, supplement by direct observation, secondary data etc.

Techniques to reduce bias: Techniques to reduce bias may include ordering questions in an open-ended way, interviewing on site without disrupting the individual's work, phrasing questions in an easily understood form, and by probing questions at length.

Cross-Checking

Gather information about a particular topic from a variety of different sources, using a variety of data-gathering methods. Also cross-check information coming from different sources.

Use of Secondary Data

Much information is likely to be a available in files, reports and with sundry individuals. Every effort should be made to collect and use all available secondary data. However, the time available to collect, compile and use secondary data is often inadequate. Furthermore, the data available may not be of the type needed.

Minimum Data Sets and Indicators

Much work is being done both on the generation of minimum data sets and the generation of minimum ndicators as a framework for information gathering. These 'sets' have been developed in response to the recognition that RRA fails most often due to the fact that important aspects of a particular issue are not covered.

However, the use of minimum data sets has evoked considerable controversy among practitioners as they very often prove counterproductive by limiting the scope of enquiry. At the same time, they help ensure that irrelevant information is not collected.

Use of Interactive Tools

Tools such as ranking games, problem-solving games, sketches of village resource-use patterns participatory assessment, transact overlays, seasonal labour calendars etc. can be used to collect information for planning through a more participatory process.

Ranking games have been used to elicit local knowledge and criteria about any phenomenon. A number of factors or alternatives are listed and the group is asked to rank them from their local criteria.

Another approach has moved away from pre-set criteria and instead elicits categories from the community members themselves against which a viable village action plan is then designed.

When groups are drawn on the seasonality of labour demands and activities, a surprisingly detailed amount of information emerges that is readily understandable.

Similarly, sketch maps, aerial photographs etc. of the village and its resource base are useful tools for interactive discussion with the villagers. Some guides to the village dialogue approach are available which may prove helpful.

RESULTS

The situation analysis report that will emerge from RRA is likely to reflect a shared multidisciplinary perspective on the needs, priorities, problems, attitudes and cost-benefits. It is also likely to reflect compatibility with the work patterns, social norms, personal preferences and social stratification of the probable beneficiaries. Since such a report is generally available in a relatively short time, the information and constraints can be kept in view while designing projects.

5

Determining Programme Objectives

All social development programmes have specific objectives. Implementation of a programme revolves around these objectives. To decide and write good programme objectives, rural development planners must necessarily understand the meaning and nature of objectives.

Objectives

According to Kelsey and Hearne (1949), objectives are expressions of the ends towards which efforts are directed. However, some educators use the terms objective, aim and purpose synonymously.

Leagans (1961) says that in reality it is not very important that we distinguish between these terms so long as we understand what is meant by them. It is generally agreed that objective means a direction of movement, for example, in which direction do you wish to go in the given area with respect to the dairy enterprise—towards greater number of dairy cattle, larger herds, fewer dairy cattle, better quality of cattle or some other possible direction.

Morris (1937) speaks of aims as being a very generalised and broad statement of direction which life on the farm should be taking with respect to given activities. For example, improvement of the farmer's economic welfare may be thought of as an aim. This may have some more specific objectives such as better feeding practices, larger size of herds, improvement of soil fertility. Some extension workers like to make a distinction between the meaning of objectives and goals. If objectives are defined as directions of movement, then a goal may be defined as the distance in any given direction one expects to go during a given period of time. For example, an objectives in a block extension programme may be to raise the average wheat yield from 40 quintals to 50 quintals per hectare. The goal then for the current year may be to raise the wheat yield by 5 quintals per hectare.

In summary, we can say that objectives as they are developed from an analysis of the situation range from the general to the specific. The general ones may be termed aims. Thus the term 'aim' is generally used in the broad sense and usually includes several objectives in it. A goal is a small part of an objective. It designates the distance to be travelled during a given period.

Levels of Objectives

According to Kelsey and Hearne (1949), it is better to use only the word objective and follow the concept that there are several levels. According to Thompson (1943), three levels of educational objectives may be recognised.

1. *Fundamental:* These are all-inclusive objectives of a society. Examples: the good life; better citizenship; democracy; better prosperity.

2. *General:* These are general but more definite social objectives. Examples: helping rural people to have better home living; helping farmers to raise their farm production.

3. *Working objectives:* These are specific objectives. They may be stated in two ways. One is from the point of view of the extension worker and the other is from the point of view of the people.

In deciding upon objectives, it is necessary to decide on the overall objectives first and then to fix the smaller ones. Each small or working objectives, when attained, contributes to the larger objective of change in behaviour.

Components of an Objective

There are at least three essential components (Fig. 3) of an educational objective:

1. Learners to be affected.
2. Behavioural changes to be effected.
3. Content or subject matter to be taught.

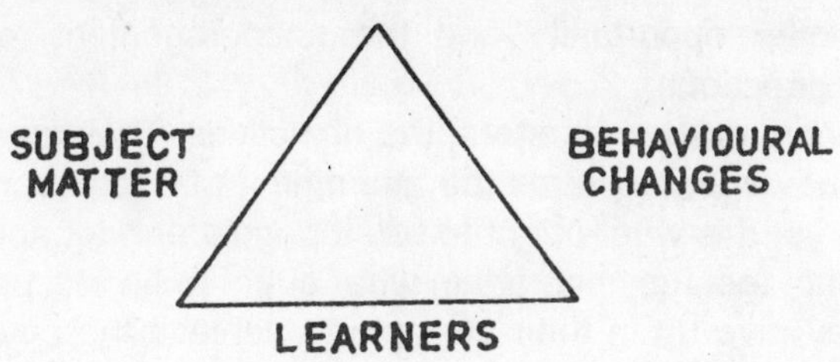

Fig. 3. Components of a programme objective

Qualities of Objectives

1. To be effective, objective must be based on research and on an analysis of the situation.

2. To be valid, they must be based on the representative thinking of the people.

3. The objectives must be attainable:
   i) through the extension education process;
   ii) within the time limitations;
   iii) within the physical resources of the learners;
   iv) within the learners' learning abilities.

4. The objectives must be significant to a relatively large number of potential participants.

5. Objectives must be clearly stated. They are the criteria for the busy extension worker for accepting or rejecting outside tendencies to encroach upon his central efforts. To the people they represent the direction of assistance towards the achievements of their goals.

6. Objectives must be stated in terms of behavioural changes in a particular subject-matter area. Changes in behaviour may be in such areas as knowledge, attitude, understanding, skill etc.

7. Objectives must be dynamic if there is to be progress and not mere evolution in the development of people. The objectives of extension programmes must be clearly and periodically deter-

mined in view of the progress and changed conditions.

8. Objectives need to have flexibility and to provide balance in the programme. Not all people desire or need to move in the same direction or equal distance. A good objective should provide for a large group of people to move in the direction they want or need to move. A balanced programme in extension should offer opportunity and the encouragement to move in several directions.

9. People must understand the objectives. They mean a direction of movement towards the attainment of a foreseen end. The foreseen end is what ought to be. If people are not able to grasp and do not feel they can attain what ought to be in a programme, they may give up in their struggle to achieve the objectives.

10. Objectives must be socially desirable.

11. Objectives must be such as can be measured or evaluated. Every teaching objectives has three aspects:

i) people to be affected;
ii) changes in people's behaviour; and
iii) content or subject matter to be taught.

Role of Objectives

Educational objectives should fill the following roles:

1. They should tell who is to be affected.
2. They should describe the kind of changed behaviour or new situation to be attained through the teaching effort.
3. They should serve as a criterion for selecting teaching methods, techniques and subject matter.
4. They should serve as a criterion for accepting or rejecting various kinds of educational activities to be carried on.
5. They should serve as a point of departure for evaluating the teaching effort.

Deciding Objectives

The objectives are decided by the programme planning committees at various levels. Factors that need to be considered while deciding programme objectives include client needs and interests emerging from situation analysis, availability of resources—both financial and organisational, overall objectives and philosophy of the organisation, and the state and national policies, directions and emphasis.

According to Beal et al. (1966) the following conditions should be met in order to decide upon good programme objectives:

1. Situation statements relative to each of the major needs and interests are determined.
2. All persons and groups required to be involved in determining situation statement have been actually and adequately involved.
3. Immediate and long-term objectives are determined for all major needs and interests.
4. Immediate and long-term goals are determined for all major needs and interests.
5. All concerned have been adequately involved in determining objectives.

Writing Programme Objectives

Programme objectives must be written in a form that they look specific and not vague. Programme objectives should be so stated that they guide those who are to implement the programme clearly and definitely. Similarly, they must be written in a form that they can be measured and evaluated.

If the programme objective, for example, is to improve the health of the children of Gujarat, it is so general that it may lead to different implementations by workers planning very different activities. However, if the programme objectives are written in the following manner, they will look specific both for implementation and evaluation.

Long-term or Five-year Objectives

1. To give the farm youth an organisation of their own by organising at least one club in each village, through which they can plan, work, develop group action, solve mutual problems, learn to abide by majority rule, express themselves clearly and make their own decisions.

2. To help member boys and girls appreciate the value of research and to apply its results in solving everyday problems in the field and in the home.

3. To provide members, boys and girls an opportunity to 'learn by doing' through planned farm and home projects, and by demonstrating to others what they have learned.

4. To develop in club members habits of healthful living and to provide them with information and direction in the use of leisure time.

5. To instil in them the elements of sportsmanship and fair play.

6. To help them develop better understanding of the dignity of labour and place of youth in the society and the contribution they make to democracy.

Objectives for the Club Members

1. Gain knowledge, skills and attitudes through real life experiences.
2. Realise the satisfaction and dignity of labour.
3. Develop leadership talents and abilities.
4. Recognise the value of research and learn decision-making processes.
5. Understand the relationship of farming to the economy and human welfare.
6. Practice healthful living and constructive use of leisure time.
7. Strengthen personal standards and citizenship ideas.
8. Cultivate desire and ability to co-operate with others.

Annual Objectives

1. To organise 20 farm youth clubs for boys separately for age groups of 12–18 years and 19–25 years in selected villages.
2. To help club members recognise the value of agricultural research and to help them learn decision-making for its application.
3. To assist club members to develop proper leadership talents and abilities.
4. To assist club members to realise the satisfaction and dignity of labour.
5. To help members to develop an appreciation of good health and the relationship of good nutrition and exercise to personal health, appearance and energy.

6

Developing a Plan of Work

A plan of work is an outline of activities so arranged as to enable efficient execution of the entire programme. It answers the questions of how, when, where and by whom the work is to be done. The action planned must include:

1. People to be reached;
2. Goals, dates and places;
3. Teaching procedures to be followed;
4. Duties, training and recognition of volunteer leaders;
5. Part to be played by extension personnel;
6. Part to be played by other agencies;
7. Plans for measuring results.

Elements

We have said that a plan of work is an outline of procedures so arranged as to enable efficient execution of the entire programme. When a statement of situation, objectives and problems has been drawn, we know what is to be done and why. Our plan of work to carry this out must tell us who, how, when and where.

Whom Shall be Reached?

Every problem appearing in the programme concerns specific people. It may include all the farmers in a block or selected ones. The characteristics, culture and location of the people we decide to reach will affect the methods we must use. Once we definitely know the total or particular group to be reached, it is possible to choose leaders within this group or leaders who can reach to serve them.

How Shall we Work?

This brings us into the field of choosing methods. Research evidence shows that changes in practices by farmers are caused by a wide variety of teaching methods. These usually require several contacts or repeated contacts to obtain results. Some extension teaching methods are good to create awareness or interest, while others are better suited to teach skill or bring change in attitude etc.

Provision for a concurrent measurement of the results in view of the objectives is necessary. Results must be measured before they can be judged for effectiveness. Through all the plans of work and the methods used, there is a constant need for co-ordination. General acceptance and smooth operation of plans will have to be ensured by forethought in giving all the concerned personnel or agencies their part in the early planning phases.

When Should we do the Work?

Timing is an important element in planning. It is therefore necessary that the various activities should be so planned as to ensure the best use of time and fullest participation by the public. Try to avoid too many peaks of work at the same time. Plan to get the attention of people for a certain problem when they are naturally faced with the problem, or are at the peak of their interest for seasonal or other reasons.

Where Shall we Work?

When an extension programme is planned for a block, all the activities included therein will extend to that area only. However, the location of the various activities depends on the distribution of the villages into various VLWs (Village-Level Workers) circles, crops, commodities, interest areas, problem areas, requests received and on the extension teaching methods to be used.

The role of each extension worker in executing the plans efficiently is largely a matter of following up the things each one did in making the plans. For each activity undertaken, the details must be worked out with the co-operating members of the staff and the people's representatives who will participate both in planning and execution. The factors that influence the efficiency of operation of the extension plans are many and varied.

Limiting factors may include:

—Lack of workers or too many workers of one type and not enough of another.

—Lack of knowledge or skill.

—Lack of judgement in selecting the most important job, or balance within the organisation.

—Inadequate or imperfect planning.

—Lack of equipment and teaching aids.

Therefore, inefficiencies may be due to fundamental faults in the structure of the extension organisation, to improper co-ordination of the different elements of the organisation or to personal inefficiencies of individual workers.

Functions

The basic function of the plan of work is to provide a guide for use in carrying on planned extension programme for the year in a systematic manner. More specifically, it should serve the following functions:

1. A specific guide for systematically carrying out all the major aspects of the planned extension programmes for the year.

2. A guide to the development of daily teaching plans and for evaluating accomplishments.

3. A guide to the timely scheduling of activities for various aspects of the programme.

Criteria for Developing

Leagans (1962) has suggested the following criteria for developing a plan of work:

1. The written programme should be suitable for use by the staff, planning groups and other individuals or groups concerned with the programme.

2. It should state the primary facts that clearly reveal the situation for major subject or problem areas.

3. It should clearly state the important problems or needs iden-

tified by the staff and the people in the programming process.

4. It should state both the long-term and short-term objectives for each major subject or problem area that is to be focused on in programme execution over a period of time.

5. It should state the objectives of the programme in a form that:

a) clearly reveals the kind of new condition or situation desired;
b) is meaningful to the staff and the people;
c) will serve as a useful guide to programme execution.

6. It should specify the subject matter related to each objective that is highly significant to the people socially or economically or both.

7. It should include the summary of the long-term programme prepared in a form suitable for public distribution, containing the following items:

a) Major facts about the overall area situation;
b) Brief descriptions of the situation, statements of major problems, long-term objectives and major means of achieving them for each of the major subject or problem areas;
c) Brief statement of the organisation and purpose of community development;
d) The names of members of the planning groups and the official staff; and
e) Other appropriate information.

8. It should be made available in a summary form to all the members of the planning groups and the professional staff.

9. It should be circulated by appropriate means so that the general public can understand its nature and objectives.

10. It should be used as the basis for developing an annual plan of work.

Specifying Learning Experiences

Suppose a programme to organise rural youth clubs in a district has been drawn with specific objectives (see Chapter 5). A plan of work may include providing the following learning experiences. It may also include where they are to be provided, when, how and by whom.

PLAN OF WORK

What	Where	When	How	By whom
1. Develop a brochure and other promotional material to create awareness of and encourage enrollment in farm youth clubs.				
2. Hold meetings in interested villages and schools with prospective members, their parents and school teachers.				
3. Organise clubs and help the members to elect their office-bearers and provide them orientation to understand the roles and responsibilities of each one.				
4. Conduct tours of club members of the experimental farms of the Punjab Agricultural University to give awareness of the value of agricultural research.				
5. Hold meetings to explore their interests and make them aware of the availability of a wide range of individual and group projects to suit their interests.				
6. Hold meetings to assist club members in considering the factors involved in project selection and provide them guidance in				

developing skills in their project. Selection and the value of careful planning and satisfactory completion of their projects need to be emphasised.

7. Provide guidance to members individually as well as in groups to help them learn both the way and the how of their project work.
8. Provide opportunities for members by way of discussions among themselves about their project work and outside experiences to develop in them a sense of inquiry, a desire to explore alternatives, set goals and measure progress.
9. Encourage members to work with their own hands and tools on their individual projects by holding discussions, paying visits, appreciating the good efforts made and by occasional follow-ups.
10. Invite members of the village Panchayat to club meetings, select a group project of community interest and help them plan and carry out the project.
11. Prepare and distribute promotional material on the needs and benefits of good health and the

relationship of nutrition and exercise to personal health etc.

12. Invite nutrition specialists from an agricultural university to club meetings to explain the value of good nutrition and the ways and means of having nutritious food within their available means.
13. Teach club members indoor as well as out-door games in teams and encourage them to practice.
14. Develop project books and explain and encourage their use by members through club meetings.
15. Hold an annual camp of all the club members of the district at an agricultural university and therein hold produce competitions, sports, debates and award prizes in individuals, teams, group projects, community work, leadership qualities and the like.

7

People's Participation in Programme Planning

Allowing and encouraging people's participation in rural development programmes is an integral part of our philosophy of life, our culture and democratic traditions and is essential to the success of such programmes. The purpose is to create an atmosphere, opportunities and motivation to develop their inherent potential, whereby they become partners in their future and improve their standard of living. In the final analysis, people's involvement should lead to a situation wherein 'people operate and the government co-operates'

The logic underlying the above is that rural people want a better life and that once the superiority of improved practices and ways of doing things is demonstrated, rural people will accept them. Furthermore, once they are assured that the outsiders have an unselfish interest in their advancement and welfare, they will accept the outsiders' guidance. It is well known that development cannot be forced upon unresponsive and reluctant people.

People's participation in rural development programmes is always likely to raise several problems. The process of decision-making may have to be slow and moderate. But as one rural leader remarked: 'If' democracy cannot afford it, what is the use of it' (Sandhu, 1965).

Need for People's Involvement

If people are to become partners in their own future, they have to be actively involved in programme planning. This concept has been accepted by extension educators and is being practised throughout the world. The basic premises underlying the concept of involving people in programme planning include:

1. Involvement of representative lay people in the planning process will speed up the process of educational change among people. By careful selection and proper involvement of lay participants in planning committees, extension multiplies the teaching effectiveness of its personnel through the indirect spread of ideas and innovations.

2. Involvement of representative lay people will result in better decisions compared to those made by the professional staff alone. The idea is that when people are provided with the real facts of a situation and with good leadership, they will identify the more critical problems with which they are faced.

3. Involvement of individuals in planning activities is a beneficial learning experience. By participation in analysis of local situations compared with the ideal, participants in planning committees are better informed and better prepared for active leadership. They also learn to approach their problems on a factual basis.

The significance of involving people in planning is emphasised by Brunner and his associates. Brunner et al. (1949) have said that there is practically unanimous agreement in all studies that the maximum involvement of potential and actual constituents in programme-building produces the best results.

However, there are experts who are critical of involving people in programme planning activities. Vandeberg (1967) has said that the primary purpose of extension programmes planning is to develop a sound, defensible and progressive programme and not the education of people. He further pointed out that in developing such a programme we should not waste the time of those participating in planning. It is thus appropriate to examine whether the extension programme be planned with or for the people.

Planning for the People

Planning for the people here refers to extension programme planning without the active participation of the people for whom it has to be implemented.

There can be two major ways of planning without the involvement of the people or the audience (as we generally call them in extension terminology).

First, the programme might be planned at the national or regional level and passed on through the extension worker to be imposed on the people for execution. Thus the people are involved at the execution stage only.

The second possibility is that the extension agency at the local level, with its technical knowledge and training in extension philosophy and methods, may think that it is able to visualise all rural people and their needs and problems and thus prepare a programme for its area. Once the programme is chalked out, the main emphasis would be to motivate people to adopt and implement it.

In both these types of approaches to planning for the people, many of the people's needs and interests would be overlooked. We have defined that an extension programme is 'a set of clearly defined, consciously conceived objectives or ends derived from an adequate analysis of a situation, which are to be achieved through extension teaching activity'.

The extension programmes conceived about would not weigh with this statement in that true and objective analysis of a situation is not done and so the programme is not based on a real diagnostic analysis of people's needs and wants. Whatever has been presumed may be just symptomatic treatment which, as all doctors know, gives no relief. Important factors related to the actual situation and opinions and experience would be neglected. As a result, the interest and belief of the people in the programme would not be strong enough to motivate them to take the responsibility of execution. 'In many situations', as Ross (1967) observed, 'it tends to manipulate ideas and people to secure the ends of a professional elite'. And as we all know, 'rural development in democratic countries is not a matter only of plans and statistical targets and budgets, technology and methods, material aid and professional staff, or agencies and organisations to administer them'. Rather, it is an effective use of these mechanisms as educational means for changing the mind and actions of people in such ways that they 'help themselves' attain economic and social improvements. Hence the process is one of 'working with people, not for them; of helping people become self-reliant, not dependent on others; of making people the central actors in the drama, not stage-hands or spectators'. Furthermore, in extension programmes we lay emphasis on education and not on service, and planning for the people would be nothing short of service while planning with the people would be nothing but educating them. It is well known that education makes people more self-reliant while service makes them dependent on others. There is still another aspect of this proposition as Alexander H. Leighton remarked: 'No matter how good a plan is, if the people for whom it is made fail to feel it belongs to them, it will not work successfully. Unless an activity is planned with them, people in free choice societies will not long participate in them.

One might say that rural people usually do not see far enough ahead to agree on future projects for the improvement of their situation. This may be true in general but they should always be prepared through discussion to see the necessity and importance for planning and adopting such programmes. Then, we may depend on their co-operation and participation in the implementation of the work.

Still one could never ignore a gross fact that to begin with, in almost all the countries of the world where extension education has been introduced, programmes were planned for the people rather than with them. Speaking in Jordan, Singh (1962) said that in Nepal an extension programme was initially framed for the people. We never asked the needs of farmers because they did not know their proper needs, problems and solutions. Nothing short of this also happened in India. Prior to the introduction of the Panchayat Raj, it was officially admitted that extension programme planning was for the people. They were involved in the execution stage. Even the study team appointed by the Planning Commission (1957) observed that 'the targets have been fixed by the district level or the block level officers without consulting the local representatives of the people'. Similar situations have arisen in Pakistan, Jordan, the Netherlands and even in America. Of course, with the proper understanding of the concept and necessity of planning with the people, and will increased professional competency, and together with overcoming some of the other hurdles in the way, greater stress is now being given to planning with the people.

Planning with the People

The experience of several countries advanced in extension work has proven that the extension programme should start from the local level. Information on local conditions and other factors related to people's attitude, manner of living, financial situation and human power facilities, should be taken into consideration in planning an extension programme. The extension worker should acquaint himself with the general agricultural, social and economic conditions of his area. He needs to do a job analysis in co-operation with groups of progressive farmers of major farm enterprises and various important rural activities in order to know the standard practices and to select the important and crucial problems. In the light of this, the programme should them be discussed with concerned people to secure their interest and to assure their maximum participation in the execution of the work. To achieve the extension's major objectives—increase in income, development of leadership among farm people, building self-reliance and decision-making, an extension worker should take the steps just mentioned in co-operation with farmers and rural leaders. This is the basic foundation for all fruitful achievement that an extension worker hopes to attain in working with rural people.

Participation of the people with the extension worker in studying local conditions helps him know exactly what their problems are, felt needs of the majority, the causes of the problems, other problems and needs that the people do not recognise and feel clearly and what has been done by individuals or groups to improve the present situation. The extension agent, by working closely with the people of his area, sharing opinions and experience, will have a better understanding of their ability and capacity to accept new ideas and practices. He may also discover some advanced persons who have already tried in some way or other the practices and new methods that he wants to introduce. These progressive individuals will be of great help to the extension worker in disseminating information and making the new practices more easily accepted by the rest of the people. Participation of the people in the preparation and planning of the programme makes the extension worker realise the limits of people's facilities and contributions to implementation of the programme. Thus he plans his work within these limitations to ensure the maximum contribution of the people concerned.

We often argue that since the majority of our people are illiterate and ignorant, what kind of contribution can they offer to programme planning? This is a false idea and wrong conception of the rural people. They may be illiterate or have a low elementary education but this does not prevent them from being intelligent and having valuable experience in their field of work. A good extension worker does not overlook the rural people's intelligence and experience. On the contrary, he must make use of them in carrying out his work. This fact has an important psychological effect on farm people. Consideration of their opinions makes them interested in the work and willing to cooperate in the implementation of the programme, feeling that it is their own programme prepared for their own benefit.

Planning an extension programme with the people has several other advantages which contribute to the achievements of the major objectives. It provides for:

1. Training people to think for themselves, analyse their own conditions, realise some of their unfelt needs and problems and to find the necessary solutions.

2. Training leaders and developing leadership among rural people who usually depend on someone else, especially government, to help and take the lead in everything.

3. Continuity of the work which falls mainly on the farmer's shoulders. The extension worker himself is not able to do all the work. The people should learn to take the responsibility of implementing different parts of the programme. Their participation in planning the programme makes them believe in it and encourages them to assume such responsibilities.

4. Making people feel that they are respected and gently treated at least in a matter which is of their own interest, especially in countries where regulations, projects and programmes are prepared at high level and imposed on people for execution. This factor is very important for extension work.

5. A democratic procedure, giving a chance to everyone to present his ideas and find his place in the overall programme. All extension objectives call for the improvement of rural areas but experience has taught us that the democratic procedure in carrying out work is the more fruitful and right way to achieve

the aims of extension. It is, no doubt, a slow process but it is a sound and sure one.

So, as Mohammad (1960) said: 'Unless people become involved in the extension programme, the programme will wither and die'. It may be concluded that initially in almost all the countries of the world, extension programmes were planned for the people. However, as soon as the extension organisations became effective, planning of extension programmes became more and more with the people. It is only when the planning is with the people that it results in real progress and development of the people. So there has been increased appreciation of the value of indigenous plans as opposed to externally imposed ideas.

Extension programmes should be planned principally from the 'bottom-up' but cannot completely exclude some downward planning due to national objectives and the human and financial resources available to the government. But participation of the people helps to arouse interest and those helping to determine a programme will usually do all they can to make it succeed. People must participate in obtaining information, analysing, deciding upon problems, objectives and solutions. The extension service must render assistance in arranging situations whereby people can easily participate, provide guidance in analysis and furnish information.

Let us therefore keep our basic philosophy in extension and plan with the people for their benefit and never for them, thereby ensuring real progress in their development and not mere evolution.

Organising Planning Committees

What is an Advisory Committee?

An advisory committee may be defined as a group of lay people organised from among the community to serve as an advisory group to the extension workers, who are responsible for the development and execution of an extension education programme at the block level. The advisory committee, whatever its form and whatever its composition and size, is inevitable and must be a part of the larger social system.

What to Expect from an Advisory Committee

A basic tenet of the philosophy of extension programme development is that extension programmes must be developed with representative people. It is generally recognised that the programmes are to be developed with the people, not for them or by them. This concept implies that in this process of developing an extension programme, there are specific roles or functions to be performed by selected lay people and certain functions to be performed by members of the professional extension staff.

As McCormick (1963) remarked: 'This approach leads us to the first basic principle that "form should follow function".' It is not very profitable to structure a group and then look for something to do. So, it seems necessary to identify what roles the advisory committee should be expected to perform in an extension setting, in order to see how best it can be structured to perform those roles.

Stogdill (1959) suggested the following as possible and logical outputs of group endeavor:

i) *Productivity*, in terms of the accomplishment of predetermined objectives and goals.

ii) *Morale*, which is a measure of the degree to which a group actually utilises its potentiality for freedom of action.

iii) *Integration*, a measure of the group's capacity to maintain structure and function under conditions of stress.

The last two products (morale and integration) directly affect the productivity or achievement of group objectives. Both of them are common for all types of structured advisory groups.

In terms of productivity, the extension advisory committees basically have the function of co-operatively planning extension programmes. Sound decisions are one of the principal outcomes sought from effective planning committees. The principal functions of planning committees are:

i) *Advisement:* This refers to the giving of advice. In this case, advisory committee members render advice to the professional staff on the situation, problems and objectives for extension work based on their interpretation of the situation.

ii) *Interpretation:* This relates to the job of the committee in looking at the facts and determining what they mean, especially in relation to what is desirable or possible.

iii) *Legitimation:* This refers to the fact that people are influenced by what others say and do. Whether the committee members approve or disapprove an idea or a practice will have its effect on the behaviour of others, particularly when the actions are communicated to others.

iv) *Communication:* This refers to the spread of ideas from the committee to the clientele they represent. Thus through participation, the committee members should receive opportunities to think, plan, help identify needs, define problems and appraise results.

Peason (1966) has said that if these functions are performed effectively by a planning committee, three important outcomes should result. One, the programme planned will be sound. Second, the diffusion of information will be facilitated. Third, the individuals who go through the process will possess knowledge about the latest technological information and be able to further develop their leadership and citizenship qualities.

CONSIDERATIONS IN ORGANISING AN ADVISORY COMMITTEE

Having set some guidelines about the expected roles of advisory committees in extension education, let us see how we can organise an effective advisory committee for achieving the best results. However, it should be borne in mind, as McCornick (1963) cautioned, that '... as is true in many social science areas, there is no known scientific procedure that will guarantee the proper combination of the various elements into an effective organism Rather it is a combination of scientific principles with a certain degree of artistry on the part of the professional worker'. This involves a careful blending of professional 'know-how' with the knowledge, values and feelings of lay people.

Hollan (1965) reported that the achievement of a committee will be the group output which results from the member inputs, mediated through structure and operations, resulting from whatever variables are present. He also noted that as many as forty-one variables affecting group outputs have been experimentally identified by psychologists. Beal, Bohlen and Raudabaugh (1965) listed the important internal dynamics of groups as: (1) atmosphere, (2) communication patterns, (3) participation, (4) group standards, (5) social control, (6) general role definition, (7) functional unit act roles of group members, (8) human relation skills, (9) heterogeneity, (10) group size and (11) group evaluation.

As Hollan (1965) remarked: 'These variables influence each other in varying degrees'. It is also to be recognised that some of these mediating variables can be controlled while others are beyond control to an appreciable extent.

Several research studies have been conducted in the area of organisation and utilisation of advisory committees in extension work. Some of the conclusions which can help to organise an effective committee for the achievement of the objectives listed above, are discussed hereunder.

Structural Form of the Committee

This will mostly depend on the kind and number of subparts and the number of members. Most informal organisations of this character tend to evolve from one form of structure to another but the evolving process should be guided toward the most desirable kind. However, the experience of several decades in extension work suggests that '... the most effective pattern appears to be one with a central body and a number of subparts which include in their membership one or more from the central unit (Fig. 4). Frequently, the subparts are standing committees like the central unit' (Marquart, 1955)

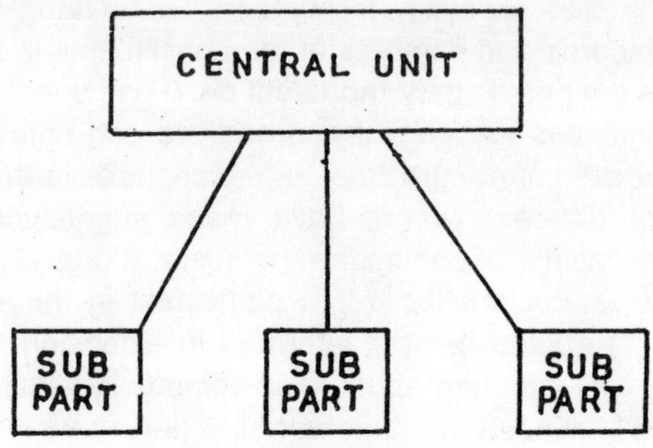

Fig. 4. A model organisation

Carter (1964) reported that the performance of County Advisory Committees was more effective when the duties, obligations and power or influence were widely distributed among the members.

Interests to be Represented

Beal et al. (1966) remarked that based on an analysis of the county situation, representatives from county and/or community or areas, committees, clubs, special interests and other groups should be organised into a committee to plan the county extension programme. The people should represent rural, urban, civic, all age groups and all socioeconomic levels. In brief, the members of the advisory committees should truly represent all relevant groups and interests. Roland (1961) had also stated that 'relevant' in this context means: (i) those with objectives that fall within the scope of extension educational responsibility and (ii) those that would be included as a part of the people in a particular context.

Do Qualifications of Members Affect Committee Outputs?

It is well recognised that the quality of an organisation depends not merely on the number of people in it, but also on the calibre of the individuals who compose it. Representativeness in an organisation means having insight into the problems of the people or a particular segment of them. It means knowing at any particular time their thoughts, their problems, their needs and their wants. This implies an ability to perceive, understand and think about the concerns and interests of the constituents in much the same way as the people they represent do. It has another dimension too. It includes the capacity to analyse and come up with solutions that are sound, practical and acceptable to the people. A number of different writers have made suggestions about needed qualifications of committee members. Biddle (1953) suggested these characteristics: (a) a participant in the extension programme (b) should be well informed in extension aims and problems (c) well informed about local community affairs and (d) organisationally minded; in other words, a person who will make contributions in committee meetings.

The question of whether or not to be represented on the committee can be left to the various potential constituent interests or groups. However, the question of qualifications should not be left to the politics of vested interests or to ill-considered selections. Each member should be able to meet as nearly as possible some predetermined qualifications.

TENURE OF ADVISORY COMMITTEE

The continuous nature of extension programmes makes a definite time element in the tenure of the membership very important. The service of members must be for a definite period in order to attract able individuals and allow them to plan productive use of their period of tenure. However, research has also shown that ad hoc committees may be quite productive albeit not very effective in group morale and integration. So the tenure should be reasonable long enough for the committee to maintain morale and integration but short enough to safeguard against a major portion of its energy being expended in carrying out routine goal-directed operations.

COMMITTEE LEADER

The smooth functioning of the committee and its success in achieving the purposes for which it was established will depend primarily on the skills and abilities of the chief officer (Chairman) and the extension worker. Carter (1964) reported that the performance of extension advisory committees was more effective when the County Agent Chairman was perceived to provide initiation of structure leadership behaviour for the advisory committees. However, their effective performance was not associated with giving consideration to leadership behaviour of the county agent chairman.

The chairman of the advisory committee is the most important single person from the extension worker's point of view. A careful study of needed qualifications before a selection is made will amply reward the extension worker and the committee for the effort expended. On the other hand, the penalties for having a poor leader on the committee are great.

NUMBER OF MEMBERS

Two major considerations enter when we think of how many

members to include in the committee. The first is how many groups or interests have been identified. The other is, what minimum number will fairly represent and accurately reflect the concerns and points of view of the identified constituent groups and interests. Size is of particular importance in deciding what group techniques to use under certain conditions to accomplish specific goals. Size is also an important variable that may limit the amount and qualify of communication that can take place between individual group members. Beal et al. (1966) reported evidence that an increasing proportion of group members indicated feelings of threat, frustration, tension and inhibition to participate as group size increased. Several research studies support the fact that as groups become larger than twelve, a trend towards factionalism becomes apparent.

Atmosphere in Committee

The importance of group atmosphere cannot be overemphasised. It is 'the pervading mood, tone or feeling that permeates the group'; for maximum participation and best results the atmosphere should be permissive, friendly and warm. It should be sufficiently supportive for the members to be able to accept constructive criticism, if necessary. When a group is attempting to complete a task, tension might begin to build up between conflicting ideas, values and attitudes. So to maintain a proper atmosphere and to keep good cohesiveness high, some maintenance roles must be played. Such roles are: encouraging, harmonising, compromising or perhaps gate-keeping.

Committee Cohesiveness

Committees are productive in proportion to their cohesiveness. Cohesiveness is an affinity, a sense of belonging, a feeling of accepting and of being accepted and can be developed only if members work, think and feel together about a real problem. If a member is unable or unwilling to change his conduct to conform to the general opinion of the group or to effect other changes in himself, some rearrangement in membership of a particular group or committee may be necessary.

Hollan (1965) has said that cohesiveness depends on whether or not the group can serve any or all of the following functions for its members:

i) fill a need for affiliation;
ii) create some aspects of reality which are meaningful to the individual;
iii) provide members with a feeling of being useful and of having contributed something of value;
iv) enhance member's feeling of social worth and success.

Social Control

This may be termed as the means whereby the group secures conformity to the expectations of its group members. This may take the form of rewards to group members for meeting group standards. Such rewards may include recognition before the group, election to office, being accorded a certain status or being given some other tangible recognition such as a perfect attendance pin.

Conclusion

The primary responsibility for having a suitable organisation for involving the people in extension work rests with the extension agent. A suitable organisation is one that meets accepted criteria for a good organisation and conforms to the policies of the State Extension Service. This fact leaves open the door for imaginative application by the agent of proven principles in establishing an organisation and evolving efficient working procedures for it. A proper understanding of (i) the individual in a group, (ii) the internal dynamics of the group and (iii) the external forces of the group can help to increasing group outputs. Although research has provided sufficient guidelines for organising an effective advisory committee, still there is no one known procedure that will guarantee the proper combination of the various elements into one effective organism.

8

Role of Specialist in Extension Programme Planning

The subject-matter specialist is a unique person in the extension service. His responsibility is that of assembling, interpreting and disseminating information that will assist people in identifying and solving the problems of everyday living in a way that is socially and economically satisfying to them.

Early in the history of the extension service, a need arose for staff members who could furnish extension workers information adopted for local use. Thus the position of a subject-matter specialist came into being. As more technology was developed and as problems of farm families became more complex, the need for additional specialists increased.

Knowledge of his particular subject area is the specialist's bulwark. To impart the information he has, the specialist functions as a teacher, a planner, a co-ordinator, whose special task is integration and working relationships. The specialist must be able to view the contribution of his teaching in the light of the teaching of others and to develop his teaching in such a way that it assists the family towards the solution of overall problems, rather than towards the solution of segments of the problem.

Thus the specialist is dependent on the work of others in extension to obtain information needed before guiding people.

Getting the information collected to the people in order to produce changes in their behaviour is not a simple process. The people must come to want the information the specialist has in order to use it effectively. They must learn something of the extent of the information available to help them achieve their goals. Making people aware of such information is part of the educational job of the extension worker. If these people are to solve their problems, there is need for determining the direction in which their behaviour will be changed. This direction much be planned in such a way as to effect the kinds of results desired by the people. Programme planning can determine the direction.

Programme planning is an educational process. It provides people the opportunity to study their situation, to identify their problems and to decide on objectives that are significant in reaching the goals they wish to attain. These people plan the direction of their efforts and determine the kinds of assistance they want from the professional extension workers when they select objectives. If the specialist is a part of the planning process, he is better acquainted with the situation of the people. He has a better understanding of the kinds of information that the people have considered in studying their problems. Consequently, the specialist has a better understanding of the significance of the objectives the people have chosen to develop He may be able to direct his teaching efforts in a more effective manner.

Specialist's Job

The job of the specialist has been described in many ways. Reid and Wilson (1933) found that their work could be listed under nine headings which would fall into four broad groups, namely, planning, training, direct teaching and studies to increase effectiveness of work. Authors such as Kelsey and Hearne (1949) and Raudabaugh (1957) have listed seven concepts of the functions of specialists. However, it is quite appropriate to identify the job of the specialist under four headings, namely, planning, teaching, co-ordination and evaluation. Of course, his primary duty is to teach and equip extension workers and people to enable them to meet the current problems and needs of farm people. This emphasis places him in the position of subject-matter authority in his field. Nevertheless his role in other areas is not less significant. His role concerning extension programme planning is described below.

Specialist as a Planner

A subject-matter specialist is expected to provide basic data upon which a programme can be developed which will assist people in solving their problems. Basic data is that information the planner uses in planning and the teacher uses in teaching. As a general rule, the data before being useful and significant must be:

i) collected from various sources; ii) analysed; iii) evaluated; iv) interpreted and put into usable form; v) adopted to local conditions; vi) popularised; and vii) simplified and clarified. This is part of the planning function that precedes the teaching job of the specialist. In a sense, the specialist is an analyser, an evaluator and an interpreter of facts.

The specialist does his own planning and assists others with their planning. 'Each specialist should prepare a comprehensive plan in which he sets forth his proposed activities and indicates the direction in which he wishes to go' (Raudabaugh 1957). This statement indicates that planning precedes action. The specialist needs to have a clear understanding of the accomplishments he wishes to attain before he can teach others effectively. At this point he is determining his own direction (he is deciding upon objectives). The direction is based in part on his successful field experience and grass-roots acquaintance with farm people and their problems. He is responsible for determining long-range objectives based on the recognition of long-range problems in his subject-matter area. These objectives should guide the work in his area over a period of years. The specialist needs to constantly plan ahead, basing his planning on changes and research developments. He develops a yearly plan of work which spells out objectives to be reached during a given year. The specialist's plan of work is based on plans of work developed by individual districts.

The specialist has the responsibility for developing plans to carry out phases of work in the various programmes. These phases may be planned with extension workers, lay leaders, other specialists, administrative and supervisory staff and members of other organisations with whom extension work is being planned. The planning may be in relation to any of the following: (1) programme planning, (2) the teaching process, (3) determining progress and accomplishments and (4) maintaining co-operative relations with other organisations. The assistance given to others in planning is a responsibility of the specialist by virtue of his knowledge of his subject matter. As planning progresses, the specialist can aid in the clarification of objectives and assist other people as well as extension workers to put their plans into action.

One of the planning phases quite often overlooked is that of advising the extension workers regarding programme planning and assisting them in the determination of objectives.

Contributions of the Specialist

The following is a listing of some contributions the specialist can make to the programme-planning process:

1. Assisting in gathering facts from various sources, by examining them critically in view of other available information and interpreting and adapting them for use in the local situation.

2. Developing means of disseminating this information in a form meaningful to the people who are doing the planning.

3. Indicating the kinds of information pertinent to the discovery of problems and encouraging collection of only that information.

4. Assisting in determining the sources of pertinent data and aiding in the development of such devices as surveys, interviews and questionnaires to obtain the data.

5. Considering the adequacy of the findings of research and surveys in making sound decisions and suggesting additional information to supplement the findings.

6. Assisting in integrating the facts bearing on the situation.

7. Helping to develop in people a keener appreciation of the effect of public policies on the local situation.

8. Assisting people: (i) in anticipating changes and new developments, (ii) in understanding their effect on the local situation and (iii) in adjusting their programmes to meet these changes.

9. Helping people to anticipate the lasting effects of new developments.

10. Giving adequate information to help people recognise their needs.

11. Helping people recognise the relative significance of working on these needs in terms of reaching their objectives.

12. Aiding in the discovery of basic problems which may move people toward their objectives in a shorter period of time with less effect but with a greater degree of satisfaction than those problems of immediate interest.

13. Aiding in anticipating the ultimate results of working on a problem as it affects the people, their attitudes and their habits.

14. Pointing out obstacles that may hold back the acceptance of improved methods in developing a particular objective.

15. Assisting in determining objectives that are not too technical, too specialised or inappropriate for the large number of people for whom the objectives are designed.

16. Helping to determine which objective or objectives would be most appropriate to work on at a given time in the programme.

17. Aiding in anticipating the length of time needed to emphasise an objective.

18. Helping to study the relation of the objective in his subject-matter area to those in other areas, to determine whether adequate attention can be given to the accomplishment of all objectives.

19. Helping to co-ordinate the objectives in his line of work with those in other lines of work and those in other programmes with which Extension Works.

20. Aiding in evaluating objectives to determine whether they are adequate, appropriate and comprehensive for achieving the results desired by the people.

21. Aiding in anticipating the end-results of an objective and in determining how far various groups of people can go in accomplishing the results.

22. Aiding in evaluating alternative methods for solving the needs to point out the advantages and disadvantages in regard to each proposed course of action.

23. Aiding in integrating the efforts in his line of work to those of people in other lines of work throughout the planning process.

This listing gives some of the ways in which the specialist can contribute to the programme-planning process. Acknowledgement is made of the fact that there are many limiting factors that do not permit any one specialist to function in all the ways mentioned and, perhaps, this would not be desirable. A balance needs to be maintained between the work of lay leaders and the professional staff.

Factors Affecting the Specialist's Contribution

Some of the limiting factors affecting the contributions the specialist can make are:

1. Lack of time on the part of all those concerned to give to the planning process.

2. Necessary training in programme building for the staff due to its size and its rapid turnover.

3. Ineffective communication among staff members due to the size of the staff, physical limitations such as distance and policies of the administration.

4. The tendency to 'bog' people down with facts.

5. The insistent need for action on the part of some staff members and lay people.

6. Inadequate number of staff members to get the planning job done.

7. Attitude of individual workers with regard to planning.

8. Keeping up to date on the subject matter.

The specialist has an important contribution to make in the programme-building process. However, there are indications that the job of the specialist needs to be evaluated by individual state staff members resulting in policies determining which responsibilities of the specialist should receive major attention, which intermediate attention and which minor attention.

9

Alternative Approaches to Programme Planning

Introduction

Planning is a process of rational decision-making wherein means and ends are related in an attempt to achieve maximum effectiveness with the least cost. However, the philosophy of extension states that means are as important as ends and in order to achieve development of the people, extension programme planning has to be done with the people, not for them. This implies that extension personnel and people's representatives study the situation, resources and technology and identify problems, decide objectives, assign priorities and finally draw up a written statement of the programme for a definite period.

The most widely accepted and used approach for achieving above objective is extension programme planning. However, from time to time several other approaches have been suggested either to improve it or as a substitute for it. The purpose here is to briefly describe some of these alternative approaches as well as the feasibility of their use.

Some of the alternative approaches suggested for planning an extension programme include programme projection; planning, programming and budgeting system; linear programming; mathematical models of social change; farming system approach; programme evaluation and review technique; critical path method; geographic information system etc.

Programme Projection

Programme projection is an expanded concept of extension programme planning. It grew out of the discussions which took place in 1955 in the Session of the Extension Committee on Organization and Policy (ECOP) of the American Association of Landgrant Colleges and State Universities. This committee concluded that the extension service must formulate more effective programme-planning principles and procedures in order to do a more effective job of helping people to determine clear-cut, long-range programmes to meet their needs. The major concern was to overcome some of the limitations of the then current programme-planning procedures.

Meaning of Programme Projection

According to Nieder (1960), programme projection means improved programme planning by looking more broadly, looking more deeply, looking longer or farther ahead and, necessarily, involving more people. Programme projection according to Lawrence (1962) is long-range programme planning by a broadly representative group of local people. It involves the logical analysis of all available information and the setting of long-range goals and objectives for the people.

Thus the core of this process is the involvement of the people served. Moreover, it looks beyond this year or next year in developing a blueprint for the future. Programme projection enlists the sound judgement of a broadly representative group of local people in deciding what their problems are and in suggesting solutions to these problems.

Objectives of Programme Projection

The major objectives of programme projection as enlisted in the *Extension Service Review* (1956) are:

1. Helping rural people to better appraise and understand adjustments which they should make or strive for, in view of the rapidly developing agricultural technology, and thereby improve their standards of farming and living.

2. Developing with local people significant long-range program-

mes designed to meet the interests, needs and major problems of the area.

3. Helping extension workers to reorient and redirect their educational programmes and services and make efforts which are more realistic and productive in the light of what farm people really want.

Characteristics of Programme Projection

Programme projection may be viewed as a method of blending scientific knowledge and experiences of local people in order to achieve more balanced and realistic long-term extension programme planning. Programme projection helps extension workers to overcome some inadequacies of former programme planning efforts, as indicated by the following characteristics:

1. It encompasses consideration of the major problems, needs and potentials as viewed by a widely representative group of the people whom extension serves.
2. It is based on the belief that people, when involved systematically in the analysis of situations, are capable of making the most intelligent decisions regarding programmes to meet their needs and to solve their problems.
3. It recognises that participation in problem analysis provides much of the motivating force to carry out the recommended programmes.
4. It is a continuous educational process, focussing attention on a significant period of years ahead in addition to yearly or short-range problems and needs of people and provides for reappraisal as conditions change.
5. It involves a thorough study and understanding of many facts about trends and potentials, pointing up opportunities that are the basis for programme decisions by the people.
6. It provides an opportunity for the people to discover other agencies and organisations, public or private, whose services can help to solve their problems.
7. It provides a more definite and scientific basis for determining programme adjustments and resources needed to carry out programme recommendations.
8. It provides a basis for determining priorities and sets objectives against which progress and change can be measured.

Programme Planning and Programme Projection

According to Lawrence (1962), programme projection differs from the ordinary type of programme planning in the following ways:

1. Programme projection is longer-range planning and is broader in scope. It is a more complete and a more balanced approach.
2. It involves the collection and interpretation of pertinent background information from local, state and central sources.
3. It is much more thorough in the study and analysis of local problems. It is more intensive kind of programme planning.
4. It usually involves more local people with a wide range of interests.
5. It makes greater effort to determine the kind of extension assistance that local people want in helping them to solve problems and to attain their goals.

Planning, Programming and Budgeting System

Definition

According to Perkins (1970), the planning, programming and budgeting system (PPBS) is a synthesis of established techniques applied to the management and control process to produce a programme budget that relates the output-oriented activities of an organisation to the input-oriented resources.

This approach lays emphasis on output of the programme rather than inputs or resources. In this technique, the planners have better information for planning programmes and for making choices among the various alternatives in which funds can be allocated to achieve the predetermined objectives, programme activities to reach these objectives, methods of evaluating the programmes and the cost of operating them. Thus PPBS involves considering alternative ways for meeting the defined objectives in terms of their cost and benefits and then deciding upon a programme alternative whereby the output will be maximal. For this purpose the concept of system analysis or cost-benefit analysis is used. These processes help programme planners to select a preferred choice among the possible alternatives.

ELEMENTS OF PPBS

Stauber (1968) defined the following elements of the PPBS:

1. A careful specification and a systematic evaluation of objectives.
2. A search for relevant alternatives, or different ways of achieving the objectives.
3. An estimate of the total costs of each alternative.
4. An estimate of the effectiveness of each alternative.
5. A comparison and analysis of the alternatives (how close does each come to satisfying the objective), seeking that combination of alternatives which promises the greater effectiveness for given resources in achieving the objectives.

PPBS ACTIVITIES

Various activities under this technique of programme planning include:

1. *Planning:* This refer to identification of current objectives and developing criteria for their evaluation. It should also include what current activities are contributing to the objectives and what other additions are needed to achieve the objectives effectively and economically.

2. *Programme structure:* When the goals, objectives and criteria for evaluations have been defined, the next step is to develop a programme that will achieve the objectives. This requires development of a programme consisting of a group of interrelated activities directed towards attaining planning objectives. This will provide a framework for budgeting and cost analysis. It will also provide decision-makers with an objective-oriented framework for analysing the programme. Thus the programme structure becomes a series of output-oriented activities. According to Perkins (1970), an important criterion to be used in this determination is that the programme structure should permit comparison of alternative methods of achieving objectives.

3. *Budgeting:* The major element of this technique is the budget document that gives the cost for achieving each objective identified. This will tie together defined objectives, programmes, cost and effectiveness and will allow selection of most preferred alternative for achieving the objectives. Furthermore, implemen-

tation of the programme is likely to reveal several deficiencies when progress results are compared. This enables planners to redefine objectives, develop new alternatives, evaluate the new alternatives and make decisions regarding preferred programme activities.

Thus funding decisions are made on the basis of programme costs and anticipated outcomes. This process helps in ascertaining whether the full costs of programme activities are justified by their outcomes or whether different approaches might be needed for doing the job more effectively or at less cost.

Advantages: Stauber (1968) listed the following advantages of using this programming technique:

1. It provides choices among the alternatives ways in which funds can be allocated to achieve the established objectives.
2. Outputs of the programme are emphasised rather than the inputs.
3. How much more would be gained or lost by way of achieving the defined objectives, through spending more or less for a particular objectives.

PPBS Use in Extension Planning

There are several concepts in PPBS that can be used to improve the extension programme-planning process. It lays special emphasis in searching several alternatives and working out the cost of all possible alternatives and selection of the best preferred course of action for achieving the objectives. Many extension programmes are being subjected to thorough review under system analysis. PPBS allows planners to make choices between competing programmes. Use of this technique is likely to improve both the quality of programme activities and utilisation of resources.

Critical Path Method

The Critical Path Method (CPM) was originally developed to solve schedule problems in an industrial setting. It is more concerned with costs of project scheduling and how to minimise them.

CPM is a technique of project management useful in the basic management function of planning, scheduling and control.

With CPM, the amount of facilities needed to complete various facets of the project is assumed to be known with certainty; moreover, the relation between the amount of resources employed and the time needed to complete the project is also assumed as known. Thus CPM is not concerned with uncertain job times as is PERT (Programme Evaluation and Review Technique). Rather it deals with time-cost trade-offs. Because of these differences, PERT is used more in research and development projects and CPM is used more in projects such as construction where there has been some experience in handling similar endeavours.

Developed in the late 1950s to aid in the planning and scheduling of larger projects, CPM is today widely used in industry and services. CPM is basically concerned with obtaining the trade-off between cost and completion date for large projects. It emphasises the relationship between utilising more men or other resources to shorten the duration of given jobs in a project and the increased cost of those additional resources.

Thus it is a deterministic rather than a probabilistic model.

It does allow for variations in job times, however, as planned and expected outcome of resource assignments.

Most jobs can be reduced in duration if extra resources are assigned to them. The cost of getting the job done may increase but if other advantages outweigh this added cost, the job should be expedited, otherwise crashed. Thus only the critical job, not all, needs to be expedited.

Schedule-related Project Costs

Project schedules can influence two kinds of costs—direct costs associated with individual activities and indirect costs associated with the project.

As originally developed, the CPM model embodied the simplistic assumption that the time-cost trade-off for an individual activity is linear. The steeper the slope of this line, the higher the cost of expediting it. A horizontal line indicates no added cost for expedition.

There is probably a minimum duration which cannot be further reduced no matter what the expenditure or resources. Similarly, slowing the job will decrease costs only up to a certain point. Thus there is some optimum project length.

The CPM specifies a method of finding out this optimum point, the least-cost schedule.

In reality, a curved line may better represent actual costs than a straight line.

To begin with, a preliminary schedule is generated in which all jobs are assigned at their early start time and with normal resources. This is the maximum length schedule. It can be reduced only by expediting one or more of the jobs at added cost. If this added cost is less than the saving in indirect costs which result from shortening the project, then a less expensive schedule can be realised. New schedules continue to be generated as long as jobs can be crashed with a net reduction in total costs.

The cost-time slope of each critical job is examined and the job with the least slope is determined. This job can be shortened with the least expense in added resources. Then the remaining critical jobs are likewise examined. If there are parallel critical paths, then one job in each must be chosen for crashing. This process is repeated until the lowest cost schedule is obtained.

What about stretching the jobs? Generally this would mean an increase in both direct and overhead costs, if the normal time has been thought of as the most efficient time. If not, it might be possible to reduce for direct activity costs somewhat by a reduction in pace.

Obviously, this technique is unsuitable for implementing the philosophy of extension education. However, some of its concepts can be utilised in improving the traditional programme planning model.

Programme Evaluation and Review Technique

PERT was developed and has been used for research types of programmes, especially when there are a number of uncertainties in the development of new technologies. This technique assumes that specific activities and their network relationship need for planning and development of a new technology have been well defined, but it allows for uncertainties in activity time.

PERT calculates the expected value of an activity duration as a weighted average of three time estimates—optimistic, most probable and pessimistic.

$$t_e = \frac{t_o + 4t_m + t_p}{6}$$

where t_e = expected time to complete a planned activity;
t_o = optimistic time;
t_m = most probable time;
t_p = pessimistic time.

PERT also calculates variability in the completion of an activity on the basis of standard deviation. However, it simplifies the calculation of standard deviation as follows:

$$S_l = \frac{t_p - t_o}{6}$$

In other words, standard deviation is one-sixth of the difference between the two extreme time estimates. Thus the greater the uncertainly in time estimates, the greater the differences in optimum and pessimistic time estimates.

Expected Length of a Critical Path

The expected length of completion of a sequence of independent activities is simply the sum of their separate expected lengths, which gives a simple means of estimating the expected length of an entire project.

PERT and CPM

PERT differs from CPM in its attempt to recognise uncertainties by using three time estimates. PERT was created as a means of planning and accelerating development of a technological innovation which had uncertainties into a model that would provide a reasonable estimate.

CPM, on the other hand, is concerned with obtaining the trade-off between cost and completion date for larger projects. Thus CPM is activity-oriented (segments of work done over a period of time) compared to PERT, which is event-oriented (a point of time). It is thus a deterministic rather than a probabilistic model.

It allows variations in job lines as planned and expected outcome of resource management. So this method is more concerned with costs of project scheduling and how to minimise them.

Other Approaches

Linear programming requires choosing production levels for each commodity in such a manner that the total profit is maximised. Thus it is more suitable in farm management than in programme planning.

The farming system approach is a philosophy rather than a methodology; it involves whole farm and human resources utilisation with diversification. The process includes diagnostic, planning, testing and dissemination stages. Although it is an improvement over linear programming, its application in extension programme planning is limited.

Similarly, GIS and the several mathematical models of social change available in the literature require expertise of a special kind and extensive use of a computer for analysing various alternatives based on pre-determined assumptions. Thus they will not match with the philosophy of planning with people, not for them. Thus the extension programme model still remains the only alternative being used by most countries.

10

Extension Evaluation

Introduction

Extension programmes are mostly funded with public money and are planned and implemented by an organisation, which in most cases is a department of a government. In order to justify the appropriation of public funds and continuing support from the people, it is necessary that their management as well as impact be properly and adequately evaluated from time to time. How to evaluate management, achievements and failures of these programmes has been a challenge to extension workers right from the time when planned extension programmes were introduced. However, 'it was when Tyler's (1950) philosophy of educational evaluation became a part of extension education that the pattern of extension educational evaluation took a more usable, understandable form.' (Sabrosky, 1966).

The word 'evaluation' has its origin in the Latin word *valēre*, meaning to be strong or valiant. Its dictionary meanings are the determination of the value, the strength or worth of something, an appraisal, an estimates of the force of or making a judgement of something.

Evaluation as applied to the field of extension education, may be defined as 'a process of systematic appraisal by which we determine the value, worth or meaning of an activity or an enterprise. It is a method for determining how far an activity has progressed and how much further it should be carried to accomplish objectives'. Thus to an extension worker evaluation means determining the results of his extension programmes in order to know the extent to which objectives have been achieved and why and what changes would be needed in case the programme is planned again, or in its implementation.

Tyler (1950) developed two basic notions regarding educational evaluation, which equally apply to extension evaluation. These notions are that the process of evaluation (i) is essentially a process of determining behaviour of the people covered under the programme and (ii) the process of determining the degree to which these behavioural changes are actually taking place. Thus extension evaluation may be said to be a process for determining behavioural changes of people resulting from extension programmes. Once evaluation became an integral part of the extension education process, extension managers started applying this process to evaluate programme planning, management and implementation aspects of extension programmes.

Definitions of Evaluation

More specific definitions of evaluation are given by persons involved in rural development programmes. While most of these definitions refer specifically to the assessment of the results of programmes of extension education, they can also be applied to the training aspect of such programmes. Some definitions of evaluation are:

1. It is a process of systematically drawing upon experience as a means of making future efforts more effective (Beaglehold, 1955).

2. Evaluation is a co-ordinated process carried on by the total system and its individual subsystem. It consists of making judgements about a planned programme based on established criteria and known, observable evidence (Boone, 1985).

3. Programme evaluation is the determination of the extent to which the desired objectives have been attained or the amount of movement that has been made in the desired direction (Boyle and Johns, 1970).

4. It is a process which enables the administrator to describe the effects of his programme and thereby make progressive adjustments in order to reach his goal more effectively (Jahada and Barnit, 1955).

5. Evaluation is a process by which the values of an enterprise are ascertained or analysed by which one is able to understand and appreciate the relative merits or deficiencies of persons, groups, programmes, situations, method and processes (Kelsey and Hearne, 1949).

6. Evaluation is an effort to learn what changes take place during and after an action programme and what part of these changes can be attributed to the programme (Klineberg, 1955).

7. Evaluation is a comparison of the situation before and after a development programme has operated within it for a predetermined period (Matthew, 1956).

8. Evaluation can be defined as the process of determining the value or amount of success in achieving a predetermined objective (Raudabaugh, 1957).

9. Programme evaluation is the process of judging the worth or value of a programme. The judgement is formed by comparing evidence as to what the programme is with criteria as to what the programme should be (Steele, 1970).

10. It is determination (whether based on opinions, records, subjective or objective data) of the results (whether desirable or undesirable, transient or permanent, immediate or delayed) attained by some activity (whether programme, part of a programme, an ongoing or one-shot approach) designed to accomplish some valued goal or objective (whether ultimate, intermediate or immediate effect or performance, long or short range) (Suchman, 1967).

11. Evaluation is the process of delineating, obtaining and providing useful information for judging decision alternative (Stufflebeam, 1971).

12. The process of determining the extent to which objectives have been attained in evaluation (Thiede, 1964).

13. The process of evaluation is essentially...determining to what extent the objectives are actually realised (Tyler, 1950).

Nature of Evaluation

1. *Evaluation is not measurement:* Evaluation is an integral part of extension education. All aspects of extension work need evaluation. Evaluation does not mean mere measuring of achievements, which is usually done after the programme is ex-

ecuted. Extension being an educational process, it is necessary to evaluate management of the programme and methods used, achievements accomplished in line with the objectives and also to determine the reasons for success or failure.

2. *Evaluation is not exactly scientific research:* When we think of evaluation as a process of collecting information as a basis for making decisions, forming judgements and drawing conclusions, we realise it has much in common with scientific research. But there is a great difference between our casual everyday evaluation and scientific research. However, the difference is a matter of degree rather than kind. Casual everyday evaluation can be placed at one end of the scale and scientific research at the other end. There are five locations on the scale with no sharp lines of distinction, i.e., casual everyday evaluation, self-checking evaluation, do-it-yourself evaluation, extension evaluation studies and scientific research.

1	2	3	4	5
Everyday Evaluation	Self-Checking Evaluation	Do-it Yourself Evaluation	Extension Evaluation Studies	Scientific Research

Types of Evaluation

1. *Self-evaluation:* This is to be carried out by every worker as a matter of routine. This requires the self-critical attitude which is so essential for extension work. By this self-critical attitude, the chances of an extension worker growing and continuously improving his professional competency become greater.

2. *Internal evaluation:* Evaluation carried to by the agency responsible for the planning and implementation of the programme. Some of the other methods for internal evaluation are: systematic use of diaries and reports of workers, planned visits of staff members to work spots, use of special questionnaires and proforma for observation and inquiry etc.

3. *External evaluation:* Evaluation conducted by a person or a committee outside the area of operation. One of the strong features of the Indian Community Development Programme is that simultaneous with its start an independent agency, namely the Programme Evaluation Organisation, was established.

Evaluation can also be classified into (i) concurrent and (ii) ex-*post facto* evaluation.

Purpose of Evaluation

The primary purpose of evaluation in extension education is to ascertain how we can improve our effectiveness as extension workers. We evaluate a total programme or major phases of it in order to determined how much progress we have made towards specific programme objectives. Evaluation is beneficial for these reasons:

1. *Programme improvement:* Evaluation is an integral part of the educational process. It is focussed on improvement of this process. By taking a critical outlook, we can discover ways and means for improving our educational efforts. Thus evaluation gives direction to continued improvement in programming. It also provides fresh data regarding situations essential for improving programming functions.

2. *Programme accomplishments:* Evaluation helps us to determine progress with any activity or job. It also allows us to assess the results of our educational efforts. Through evaluation, we can assess the strength, weakness and value of our extension programmes. It serves as a periodic check on the effectiveness of extension activity and teaching methods used. Thus evaluation helps to determine the degree to which specific objectives are being achieved and in the process, also helps to clarify these objectives.

3. *Public relations:* Evaluation provides realistic information to report to the public, parliament and legislative bodies. Organisations, individuals and professional groups in the community need to be constantly informed regarding the extension programme.

4. *Professional growth:* Evaluation enhances our knowledge. It gives us an index as to how we are doing as professional workers. Hence we learn when we evaluate and thereby can rectify our shortcomings.

5. *Professional security:* Evaluation provides us with information that gives us satisfaction, a feeling of accomplishment, confidence in ourselves and in the extension education function. It also gives satisfaction to extension workers, Panchayat Samiti members, leaders and other staff members.

6. *Effective workmanship:* Evaluation gives us the opportunity to work together as an extension staff to determine the effectiveness of our educational programmes.

7. *Impact of extension programmes:* Evaluation helps to determine the short-term and long-term impact of the extension programmes in terms of social and economic dimensions.

8. *Content of the programmes:* Evaluation enables determination of whether the content is contributing to the overall objectives of extension or not.

9. *Methods of extension teaching:* Evaluation provides information as to whether the extension teaching methods are being used effectively or not, or whether any non-extension methods are being used etc. It also helps in involving new methods of extension.

Thus the purpose of extension evaluation is to discover the extent to which programme objectives are being achieved, to determine the reasons for specific successes and failures, to uncover principles underlying a successful programme, to direct the course of a programme with techniques for increasing effectiveness, to redefine the means to be used for attaining goals and to obtain continuous support, satisfaction and improvement.

What can be Evaluated

Where does evaluation fit into an extension education programme? Evaluation is not merely a part of all phases of extension teaching but concomitantly an analysis of the activities leading towards the results. There is need to evaluate each of the following:

1. Programme Planning
2. Programme Management
3. Programme Results

Evaluate Programme Planning

As a result of experience, theory, research and experimentation, much information has been accumulated about how an extension programme should be planned. Progress in science and technology and the broadening of extension's clientele with the accompanying great variation in needs and interests have made the scientific planning of extension education programmes more important than ever before. There is considerable agreement on certain criteria which, if followed, make for successful extension programme planning at different levels. These criteria represent the ideal with which to compare our practices and procedures or programme planning. Some of the steps needed to evaluate programming function in view of these criteria include:

i) Identify the evidence needed to form a judgement about each criterion.
ii) Specify the methods that will be used to obtain the evidence, such as personal observation, personal interview or through a systematic survey.
iii) On the basis of the evidence gathered, judge whether or not each criterion is being adequately satisfied in the programme planning activities.

Evaluate Programme Management

Carrying out an extension programme is the process of carrying through planned activities which include learning experiences specified in the plan of work. Learning experiences are provided through various teaching methods and activities, such as demonstrations, meetings, field days, radio and telecasts, newspaper articles and individual contact with the farmers.

The following list of criteria has been identified from the extension education literature and can be beneficially used in measuring our effectiveness in managing the programme implementation:

i) Appropriate groups and organisations are involved in carrying out the programme.

ii) Volunteer local leaders who assisted in carrying out the programme are given adequate training by the extension staff to do the job assigned.

iii) The subject matter presented is current and appropriate to meet the programme objectives.

iv) The methods and materials used to present the subject matter are varied and stimulating and at the educational level of the people being taught.

v) A variety of co-ordinated and integrated methods are developed to accomplish each programme objective.

vi) Audio-visual materials are clear, concise and effectively used in presenting the subject matter.

vii) Appropriate human and material resources are used in carrying out the programme.

viii) District and state staff members understand specific functions and responsibilities in carrying out the programme.

The steps that need to be undertaken to measure our effectiveness relating to each of the above criteria include:

i) Identify the evidence you need to gather about the criteria.
ii) Work out methods for collecting the evidence.
iii) List procedures for analysing and using the evidence collected.

Evaluate Programme Results

Results of an extension education programme must be evaluated in relation to the programme objectives. Programme objectives are used to evaluate accomplishments in the same manner that criteria are used in evaluating the plan and carrying out the programmes. The following steps can be used as a guide in carrying out evaluation of results:

i) State the specific objectives to be evaluated in operational terms so they are measurable.

ii) Collect evidence from the specific groups you are trying to teach.

iii) Obtain valid and reliable evidence.

iv) Select appropriate methods for collecting evidence, such as observations, personal interviews, mailed questionnaires, group interviews and the like.

v) If the total population cannot be included in obtaining evidence, be sure a sample is selected that adequately represents the whole population you are trying to teach.

vi) Draw only those conclusions about the programme that can logically be derived from the evidence collected.

While it is much more desirable to determine the behavioural changes in people, this kind of evidence is often difficult to obtain. At times, it may be necessary and desirable to measure accomplishments in terms of the learning experiences provided. This will mean evaluating specific extension activities organised for carrying out the programme. In general, the more and better opportunities the extension worker provides, the more likely the objectives will be realised. However, it is highly dangerous and frequently erroneous to assume that there is a direct relationship between the number of extension activities organised and the effectiveness of a programme in terms of achieving objectives.

Contribution of Evaluation to Programme Planning

The process of evaluation has a direct bearing on good programme building and programme execution. According to Kelsey and Hearne (1949), it makes the following contributions to extension programme planning:

1. Evaluation helps to establish a 'bench-mark'. The first principle in programme building is to get the facts about a situation and the first measurement in evaluation must be taken at the point where people start or just before the teaching process begins.

2. Evaluation shows how far our plans have progressed. Studies of extension work have shown that it often takes years of constant teaching to ensure general adoption of practices. If a practice is really good, we should push it until it is well established but take care to stop at that point and take up a new one.

3. Evaluation shows whether we are proceeding in the right direction. It helps to test our objectives and to recommend changes where needed. By its systementic approach, it may point out omissions or suggest entirely new directions of effort. It helps to focus work directly on the needs, interests and desires of the people.

4. Evaluation indicates the effectiveness of a programme. After all, the end-product of our work is to produce educational or material changes. Any good teaching plan must include the process of evaluation.

5. Evaluation helps to locate strong and weak points in any programme or plan. Improvements can be made only when we locate the weak points and make an effort to strengthen them. This applies to both planning and teaching.

6. Evaluation improves our skill in working with people. In programme building, much skill is required to enable people to bring all the facts together and to arrive at sound conclusions without domination by professional workers.

7. Evaluation helps to determine priorities for activities in the plan of work. As extension becomes more complex, one of its greatest problems is to determine what to do, how much to do and what to omit.

8. Evaluation brings confidence and satisfaction to extension work. Volunteer leaders, even more than paid workers, benefit by the satisfaction they get from knowing what results are obtained. When the evaluation shows a negative result, we can then change our work in line with what has been found and proceed with confidence. With the results of evaluation studies, rural people can more intelligently participate in future planning of their own programmes.

Evaluation Principles

1. Evaluation of a social programme should be in terms of the objectives of the programme.
2. Evaluation should include assessment and appraisal of both the product and the process.
3. Evaluation should be a continuous process, not just a point-in-time judgement.
4. Evaluation should be made by teams comprising professionals, social scientists and client representatives.
5. Evaluation should be made not only on the basis of what has been done, but also on what should have been done.
6. Evaluation should be done in the context of an organisation's philosophy and objectives.
7. Evaluation, like planning, should take place at multiple levels.

Characteristics of Evaluation Information

1. The objectives of an extension programme must be stated in clear and measurable terms. Only then can relevant and specific evidence be collected and analysed to determine the management and the successes and failures of the programme for achieving its objectives.
2. Instruments of measurement for collecting evaluative information must be very carefully designed. Not only should they be valid, but contain specific indicators to ensure that relevant information is collected.

3. Information or evidence collected for evaluation purposes must be reliable. Reliability refers to the extent to which the information collected is dependable; the extent to which there is faith in what it indicates.
4. Evaluative information must also be valid. Validity means the extent to which the data measures what it is supposed to measure.
5. Another essential characteristic of evaluative evidence is its objectivity. It refers to the extent to which the same information would be provided, regardless of who asked for it, or collected it, and the extent to which the information would be interpreted in the same way, regardless of who did the interpretation. In other words, personal bias must not be allowed to affect the data.
6. Evaluative information should be of practical use. In other words, evaluation should be done in such a way that its findings or conclusions could be used for improving the programme planning, management and impact.

Extension Evaluation Process

There are several models of evaluation available in the literature. However, a very simplified version of most of these models may be quite workable for evaluating extension programmes since, as Bhatnagar (1987) has pointed out, any extension evaluation process has to be based on certain assumptions. For example, if some inputs are provided in the form of a programme, specific outputs can be expected and if these outputs happen, then the purpose of the programme can be achieved; if the purpose is achieved, then the development goal is realised. This means that evaluation has to be so designed that the quality-types and adequacy of the input measures, outputs and their impact in achieving the programme objectives have to be evaluated systematically. The various steps involved in an extension programme evaluative process may be as follows:

Formulate Evaluation Objectives

Specific objectives to be achieved through the evaluative process must be clearly and adequately identified and started.

All further efforts should be knit around these objectives.

Classify Programme Objectives

It is assumed that each extension programme, when formulated and implemented, will have specific well-defined objectives. Since evaluation is basically a process of determining the extent to which various extension teaching activities were organised and managed and the extent to which they contributed to achieving the goals, programme objectives must be clearly understood and if necessary, further broken down into measurable terms. This is a crucial step as all further efforts will be directed towards collecting evidence related to these objectives.

Identify Indicators

To identify indicators or the kind of evidence necessary to evaluate achievement in relation to specified programme objectives, it is necessary that specific beneficiaries of the programme be identified, the kind of behavioual changes expected in them be clearly stated, and the kind of learning experiences expected to be provided to them spelled out, together with the level of management to be achieved for provided those learning experiences are specified. Once this is done, identification of specific indicators to measures the achievements will not be difficult.

For example, if the programme objective is to introduce sunflower cultivation in a given area, one level of indicators would be to determine the types of extension activities provided and their effect on changing people's attitude, knowledge and adoption behaviour. Indicators will also include the area planted, varieties grown, the recommended agronomic practices followed, the problems faced and the yield and income obtained.

Decide the Kind of Information Needed

Once the indicators for evaluating the management and performance of a programme have been indicated, specific information to be collected may be worked out. Since there is usually more information than an extension worker can collect, he has to be very discriminating about the kind and amount of information that should be collected. Timing for collection of information may also need to be specified.

SAMPLING

The purpose of sampling is to take a relatively small number of units from a population in such a way that the evidence collected from them becomes representative evidence of the entire population. Although there are several sampling methods, perhaps stratified sampling procedures may be most suitable for extension evaluation studies as they allow inclusion of all interested groups and ensure enough heterogeneity in the sample.

DECIDE THE DESIGN OF EVALUATION

An ideal design of evaluation may be an experimental one. This would allow separating the effect of the programme from other factors, by setting control and treatment groups. Several experimental designs, such as one-group pre-test-post-test design, static group comparison, pre-test-post-test control group design, Solomon four-group design, longitudinal study design, etc. are available in literature and can be used. However, in actual practice, extension programmes are seldom run in a way that allows an experimental design of evaluation. In Pilot Projects, it might be possible to use an experimental design of evaluation.

By and large, a survey method is used. This method can be used for evaluating ongoing progress or as an ex-*post facto* evaluation of the programme after it has completed its tenure.

COLLECTION AND ANALYSIS OF EVALUATION EVIDENCE

There are many methods for collecting information for evaluative purposes, such as the mail questionnaire, personal interview, distributed questionnaires, group interviews, case studies, systematic field observations, systematic study of secondary data etc. Selection of the right kind of data collection method will depend on the objectives of the evaluation, kind of information needed, time and resources available and the type of respondents from whom information is to be collected.

However, whatever the method used, a specific questionnaire or interview schedule or data recording sheet must be developed with care.

Once the data is collected, it must be tabulated, summarised and analysed with adequate care. This step should not be rushed. To avoid delay, however, analysis may be done with the help of a computer.

Interpretation of the results in a proper way is very crucial as evaluation results can be misused also. Once tentative generalisations are arrived at, it may be appropriate if they are informally discussed among the interpreters as well as with programme planning and implementation officials, so that the results of evaluation are put in a proper perspective.

The evaluation results must clearly state the achievements, failures and future adjustments needed. A written report of the evaluation findings should be prepared and made available to all concerned.

11

Research in Extension Programme Planning

Very few studies of Indian origin have been reported in the area of extension programme planning. Those available to the author are reviewed here.

Aspects Covered

A review of the objectives shows that research in this area has been concerned with the following aspects:

1. Identification of principles and procedures of extension programme planning.
2. Identification of the role expectations of extension workers.
3. Measurement of the knowledge of extension workers about various concepts related to programme planning.
4. An appraisal of the procedures followed in planning an extension programme.
5. People's involvement and contribution in the planning of extension programmes.
6. Difficulties of planning effective agricultural extension programmes.
7. Planning and effectiveness of farm production plans.

Methodology Used

Research methodology used in almost all the studies conducted in this area in India has been rather superficial. The identification of principles and procedures of extension programme planning has been based on the literature. No attempt has been made to standardise them. Neither has any attempt been made to experiment with any set of procedures or model to test their validity or relative efficacy. None of the authors have tried to identify a set of conditions or criteria that should be met in order to fulfil the requirements of a particular principle or procedure.

The understanding of extension workers regarding this concept has been measured by preparing a standard scale. It would have been better had the procedures suggested by Bloom (1960) been followed for developing a standard scale to measure the perception of extension workers about this concept. Although good attempts have been made to appraise the extent to which the procedures are currently being followed at the block level for planning extension programmes, yet they are far from satisfactory. First, in the absence of a standardised set of criteria that should be met in order to fulfil the requirements of a particular set of procedures, their validity remains to be ascertained. Secondly, appraisal has been done only on the basis of opinions expressed by the respondents. So the results are reliable and valid to the extent that the respondents were honest, competent and clear. Since the knowledge of extension workers about extension programme planning has been found to range from partial to adequate, the validity of the opinion of an extension worker about the extent to which the requirements of a particular step have been met can easily be doubted. Again, in the absence of a standard statement about the role expectations of the various extension workers involved for planning a programme at any given level, a study of their role performance would not be proper.

The aforesaid shortcomings are not only applicable to the researches done in India, but are equally true of the American studies in this area. There is therefore a great need not only to do a large number of depth studies in this area, but also to develop and standardise more valid research techniques.

Major Findings

Identification of Principles

Sandhu (1965) has identified the following set of principles of extension programme planning applicable to Punjab conditions:

i) Extension programme planning is based on analysis of the facts in the situation.
ii) Extension programme planning selects problems based on needs and interests of local people.
iii) Extension programme planning determines definite objectives and solutions which offer satisfaction.
iv) Extension programme planning has permanence with flexibility.
v) Extension programme planning has balance with emphasis.
vi) Extension programme planning has a definite plan of work.
vii) Extension programme planning is an educational process.
viii) Extension programme planning is a continuous process.
ix) Extension programme planning is a co-ordinating process.
x) Extension programme planning provides for evaluation of results.

IDENTIFICATION OF PROCEDURES

Sandhu (1965) developed the following model for planning an agricultural extension programme at the block level under Punjab conditions:

I. An Organisation for Planning
II. Planning Process:
    i) Reach understanding regarding principles, procedures, roles and time schedule.
    ii) Analyse situation.
    iii) Determine objectives.
    iv) Select problems with due regard to priorities.
    v) Find solutions.
III. The Planned Programme
    Prepare a written statement of:
    i) situation;
    ii) objectives;
    iii) problems; and
    iv) solutions.
IV. The Plan of Work:
    Prepare a plan of work containing information regarding:
    i) people to be reached;

ii) goals, dates and places;
iii) teaching procedures to be followed;
iv) duties, training and recognition of leaders;
v) roles to be played by extension personnel; and
vi) roles to be played by other agencies.

V. Execution of the Plan of Work:
i) Make advance arrangement for inputs and teaching aids.
ii) Interpret the approved programme to the staff and people's representatives.
iii) Carry out the planned programme, phase by phase, in a co-ordinated manner.

VI. Evaluation of Accomplishments:
i) Do concurrent evaluation.
ii) Do ex-*post facto* evaluation.

IDENTIFICATION OF ROLE EXPECTATIONS OF EXTENSION WORKERS

Sharma (1968) identified the following role expectations of the Agricultural Extension Officers for the planning of an agricultural extension programme at the block level:

1. Set up agricultural production committees at the village and block level to ensure people's participation.
2. Settle and ensure an agreement of all concerned officials and non-officials on principles to be kept in view in planning agricultural programmes for the block.
3. Prepare time schedule of different agricultural extension and development activities.
4. Collect information regarding basic agricultural situation in the block.
5. Analyse the basic agricultural data for identifying major problems.
6. Assist the 'standing committee No. 2' of the Panchayat Samiti in establishing priorities based on major problems, felt needs and interests of the people.
7. Allocation or resources for programme execution on the basis of established priorities.
8. Help the Panchayat Samiti to determine objectives of agricultural extension and development programmes of the block.

9. Prepare annual plan of work of the block agricultural programmes.
10. Explain the approved agricultural programmes to the block staff (village level workers and other concerned extension officers).
11. Publicise the approved agricultural programmes to the people in the block.
12. Make advance arrangements for teaching aids, supplies and equipment to carry out the approved programmes.
13. Co-ordinate the efforts and resources of other agencies and groups for promoting agricultural extension and development programmes at the block level.
14. Evaluate the accomplishments and progress of agricultural programmes of the block concurrently and at the close of the year.

Knowledge of the Concept

Sandhu (1965) studied the perception of block-level extension workers, including Village-Level Workers (VLWs), Agricultural Extension Officers (AEOs) and the Block Development and Panchayat Officers (BDPOs) about the concept, principles and procedures of extension programme planning. He found that perception was high in the case of BDPOs but medium in the case of AEOs and VLWs who, in practice, were mainly responsible to take the initiative, involve and guide the Panchayat Samiti members in extension programme planning. Their knowledge of this aspect must be increased by modifying the preservice training and by providing opportunities in the post-service training.

Extent to which Planning Procedures are Followed

Sandhu (1965) and Sandhu and Sohal (1966) found that although all the eleven steps needed for planning an agricultural extension programme at the block level had been undertaken to varying degrees, mostly the BDPOs and the AEOs did the job. The VLWs were associated only in seven. Even in these steps their involvement was from low to medium. Thus the requirements for most of these steps, except one, were not adequately fulfilled.

People's Involvement and Contribution

Sandhu (1965) and Sandhu and Sohal (1966) concluded that people's representatives were not being involved properly and adequately. The Panchayat Samiti members were associated only in five of the eleven steps for planning a block agricultural extension programme. Even in these steps their involvement was low. In other words, they were kept as far away as possible unless the statutory conditions so warranted. Thus they were mostly being used as rubber stamps.

Mehta (1966) studied the farmers' involvement in farm planning and concluded that the nature and frequency of the urgent contact, the place and number of visits made, the type of assistance given and the attitude of the agents towards the farmers were the main factors that persuaded them to adopt the plans. On the contrary, it was observed that financially well-off farmers have a tendency to allocate their resources to avenues other than planning.

Brar (1966) found that *sarpanches* contributed significantly to the planning and execution of some aspects of agricultural extension work, such as *pohli* eradication, compost work, drainage work, rat killing, control of pests and diseases, use of fertilisers, introduction of improved implements, wasteland reclamation, control of wild animals, improved seeds, green manuring and tree plantation. In the planning and execution of these programmes, the contribution of *sarpanches* was 34.32% of what was expected of them.

Difficulties in Planning Effective Programme

Sandhu (1965) concluded that the major difficulties in the way of following effective and adequate procedures of planning an extension programme at the block level in Punjab were rigidiy allocated budget, ambiguous, frequent and conflicting instructions from above, outside interference and limited training opportunities.

Planning Effective from Production Plans

Singh (1966) reported that the farmers felt that preparation of farm production plans helps in getting improved seeds and fertilisers and credit facilities. About 68% of the farmers complained about lack of technical guidance. Each felt that a duplicate copy of the plan should be left with farmer concerned.

Programme Planning Research Abroad

Identification of Planning Concepts

Several studies have focussed on identifying, describing and legitimising principles, theories and concepts inherent in the programme planning process (Boyle, 1958; Williams, 1959; Hill, 1959; Norby, 1961; Kincaid, 1962).

Identification of Extension Programme Planning Principles

Williams (1959) identified eight principles from a review of the literature. Briefly stated, these principles suggest that extension programme planning should (i) be a continuous educational process that helps develop knowledge, skills and attitudes of the participants; (ii) provide opportunities for democratic participation of the people for whom the programme is intended; (iii) be based on analysis of technological, sociological and cultural facts applicable to the people and the situation; (iv) provide for the identification of needs and interests of the people; (v) provide opportunities for participants to establish both long-time and short-time objectives and goals; (vi) provide for the co-ordination of educational efforts, activities and resources of interested leaders, organisations and agencies; (vii) be flexible enough to provide for adjustments to changing situation and (viii) include plans for evaluation.

Kapanigowda (1961) in a similar effort identified thirteen generally accepted principles of extension programme planning. These principles are: (i) programme planning should be based on conditions that exist; (ii) programme planning should be based on people's interests and needs; (iii) programme planning should be viewed as an educational process; (v) programme planning is a continuous process; (vi) effective programme planning procedure is consistent with that used in a representative democracy; (vii) effective programme planning should include local participation; (viii) programme planning should include the aid of local agencies; (ix) the county extension programme should be planned by the local people and the county staff; (x) a county extension programme must be based on adequate written long- and short-term plans; (xi) programme planning should be flexible to permit adjustment to changing conditions; (xii) effective programme planning develops local volunteer lay-leadership and (xiii) well-formulated programme planning will include and involve definite procedures for evaluation.

Isaacson (1960) listed four implications for progress in agricultural extension work: (i) extension programme should conform to its major function of education as stated by the Smith-Lever Law; (ii) where possible, the extension programme should be related to the goals as redefined in the 'Scope Report'; (iii) an extension programme developed by a representative county committee is usually the most effective and (iv) a good county extension programme should be based on the needs and interests of the people.

Identification of Extension Programme Planning Procedure

Bilokury (1958) observed that basic procedures in extension planning are: (i) analysis of the situation and problems; (ii) determining objectives; (iii) selecting appropriate teaching methods and techniques and (iv) establishing subject matter content, evaluating results and re-examining the situation to make necessary adjustments and adoption in future programme plans.

Settlemyer (1958) in his report observed that the first step in extension programme planning is preparation of the county staff. All staff members must develop a common understanding of the concepts of programme planning. The staff members study and agree on the principles involved; together they decide that programme planning is practical, useful and that the time and effort devoted to it will yield worthwhile results. The second step is to recruit and demonstrate to a planning committee the usefulness and practicability of planning. The third step is to guide the committee in the development of a long-range county programme (i.e., programme projection). Evaluation of the previous effort will point the way to overcome its defects and reveal strength upon which to base new effort.

Isaacson (1960) identified from a review of extension education literature five main elements of extension programme planning, namely: (i) organisation and process; (ii) the planned programme; (iii) the annual plan of work; (iv) programme action and (v) programme accomplishments. In implementing these five elements, the author says: 'In a democratic society, it is important that a representative group be used and that all activities be conducted in a democratic manner'.

Kapanigowda (1961) in his library study observed that no one set of planning procedures has been followed by extension workers in the United States. Planning procedures, he says, must be flexible and adjustable to fit local situations if they are to be based on the interests and needs of extension clientele.

Kincaid (1962) utilised the findings of the research studies already conducted and formulated a model for the planning process. He later (1964) conducted another study to legitimise the model and received a high level of support from the Minnesota extension respondents.

CHANGES IN EXTENSION PROGRAMME PLANNING PROCEDURES

Settlemyer (1958) observed that programme planning as well as other extension methods must be as modern as the subject matter taught.

Bilokury (1958) concluded that changes in planning procedures should be made gradually.

PERCEPTION OF EXTENSION PROGRAMME PLANNING BY EXTENSION WORKERS

Beavers (1962) developed four overall functions and 31 'Understandings, knowledge or skills' of extension programme planning and asked 104 randomly selected county extension agents whether or not these were important to their role. Ranking of the four functions was as follows: Develop an extension programme based on the problem identified co-operatively by the people and the extension staff (99%); develop further leadership abilities among those involved in programme planning committees (74%); provide the situation for people to take action in regard to problems identified (84%); and provide a basis against which the accomplishments could be evaluated or measured (81%).

Ranking for the 10 top understandings of programme planning

were: (i) understanding of the objectives of programme planning (95%); (ii) understanding of the development and execution of programme plans (94%); (iii) knowledge of basic facts about the county (95%); (iv) understanding of their own responsibility in programme planning (99%); (v) recognition of the importance of programme planning as a means for helping to improve the economic conditions of the county (93%); (vi) recognition that an analysis of programme achievements is necessary in order to effectively plan an extension programme for subsequent years (92%); (vii) understanding the importance of the ability to get others to discuss their needs and concerns and the development of that ability (83%); (viii) willingness to inform others about the programme attained through the extension programme (81%); (ix) willingness to participate in the extension programme and actively assist in carrying it out (85%) and (x) familiarity with dependable sources of information from which facts about the county situation could be obtained (79%).

Several other research studies (McCormick, 1959; Price, 1960; Clark, 1960; Villalobos, 1962; Kincaid, 1964) found that there is a lack of common understanding among extension personnel regarding programme planning objectives, policies and procedures and suggested the need for ongoing training in this area.

Edwards (1962) and Blackburn (1964) found a relationship between extension workers degree of participation in the programme-planning process and their general understanding of various concepts of programme planning. Similarly, studies conducted by Edwards (1962), Holhubner (1962), Farnsworth (1963), Guame (1963), Straughn (1963), Wallace (1963) concluded that unless the roles and responsibilities regarding programme planning are clearly defined, a great deal of confusion will continue to prevail among extension workers.

Methods of Extension Programme Planning at the County Level

Matthews (1952) studied the methods and procedures of extension programme planning being used in the United States. Generally the people in the States expressed themselves as being in favour of having 'a representative county committee plan a county program after problems and needs have been discussed at community meetings'. There were 3038 county programmes developed by this method, constituting more than developed by any othér method.

The second most popular (having been used for 2829 county extension programmes) is the method of 'discussion of problems and drafting of a program at the county level by selected representatives from townships or communities and representatives from organizations and agencies, serving as a county program-building committee.'

'Discussions of problems and drafting of a program by a county committee which is not representative geographically or by major interest' was the third method in order of number of integrated programmes developed, namely 1550.

'Program largely planned by the agents through personal consultation with leaders and well-informed people of the county not organized into a program planning committee' was the fourth popular method in sequence, through which 1002 programmes were developed.

The fifth method of determining a county extension programme was found to be that in which 'agents plan the program from their own knowledge, after a mail survey or by selection from a list of projects prepared at the College'. Only 491 county programmes were determined by this method.

Sixth in order according to the number of county programmes determined in the method named 'Program determined by commodity or special-interest committees, not organized as a county program planning group'. Through this approach, only 489, i.e. 5% programmes were determined.

The largest percentage of agricultural extension programmes i.e. 35.4%, were prepared by the second method described above and the lowest (4.8%) by the fifth method.

Vail (1953) studied the methods and procedures used in the development of agricultural extension programmes in Coahoma County, Mississippi. Of the 51 county agents surveyed, 50 had some form of county agricultural programme planning in action; all were considered to have a good action programme; 39 agents had one overall county extension programme; 45 said the people would continue with the programme regardless of extension personnel turnover.

Fifty per cent of the agents said that the programme-planning group decided the problems to be worked out during the year; 42 said problems were worked on in the order of their importance and 40 said the programme committee decided when a problem had been solved or should be moved to a different place in order of importance.

In 30 counties, goals were established to reach objectives and in 21 jobs to be done were listed. Results were checked at the end of the year in 45 counties; in 33 they were checked by both programme-planning groups and extension workers. The county programme-planning group determined objectives in 50 counties and business groups co-operated in 43 counties in developing the county programme. In 32 counties, the plan of work was made by the county programme-planning group and extension workers. The plan of work was made after the county programme was developed in 41 counties and followed through by the agents in 49 counties.

Collection and Use of Background Information in Extension Programme Planning

Whiteman (1952) in his investigation found the following information needed by the extension workers for planning block extension programmes: recommended production methods, results of local demonstrations and practices, farm family needs and desires, trends in livestock and crop productions, land-grant colleges, extension programmes, past block extension programmes, long-time agricultural programmes, number and size of farms in the block, agricultural economic outlook, land ownership in the block, land-use classification, farm and home records, available market and health facilities.

The study indicated that committee men planning block agricultural extension programmes considered information of a social and educational nature, such as educational facilities and expenses, recreative facilities, source of reading matter and churches, more valuable than did the extension personnel.

In the same study, the following information was found to be 'good' to have for planning programmes but was not considered essential: legislation affecting agriculture, educational facilities and expenses, rural housing and building needs, soil conservation district reports and programmes of other organisations, farm credit available, international relations, recreational facilities, taxes, sources of reading matter and churches.

Farmer (1959) found that 88% of her 295 respondents, who were county agents, used factual information to determine the county situation; 82% to determine problems; 74% for informing local people and 68% for building plans of work to solve problems. Half or more used factual information for integrating total county programmes and programme evaluation.

Similarly, several studies (O'Connell, 1961; Voorhees, 1960; Norby, 1961) have reported that the data collected is not adequately analysed and interpreted and that programme-planning committees follow no systematic plan in identifying problems.

The major source of information in these areas is a census, followed closely by local people. Information is collected mainly through personal contacts and observations.

Difficulties Affecting county Extension Programmes

Sprowls (1959) identified the major problems in conducting organised programmes, as seen by his respondents (county extension agents), as: (a) indecision as to direction to follow; (b) financial problems; (c) need for additional staff: (d) inadequate supply of local leaders and (e) lack of definite programmes.

Work done Abroad Regarding Organised Participation of People in Extension Programme Planning

Why organised participation ?

Thelan's (1958) experience in dealing with community disorganisation suggests effects that might result from bringing together people from a community in other types of situations. He assured that communication results from shared perceptions. Biddle (1953) has said that a 'competent community educator... should not be satisfied until he obtains active participation in an ongoing program'. The values he attributed to participation are (i) to develop attitudes favourable to community improvement, (ii) to gain support, (iii) to develop eagerness (of the citizens) to serve and (iv) to achieve unity of purpose in the community.

Houle (1961) stated five values of boards, namely: (i) to provide an opportunity for the use of collective wisdom; (ii) to secure support in the general community; (iii) to provide for continuity of policy and programme; (iv) to provide a means of preserving the democratic spirit and (v) to serve as a means of constantly training new leaders for our society.

Regarding the motivational effect of participation, Koontz and O'Donnell (1955) have said: '... among the ruling forces of human motivation are status and feelings of belonging, accomplishing and participation. Persons who have had a part in the planning or the making of a decision are certain to feel more enthusiastic in accepting and executing it. Even though the individual may have contributed little to the plan or the decisions, the very effect of participation makes him feel that it is his.'

Some research with small groups throws additional light on the advantages of participation. Beginning with a theory that resistance to change is a combination of individual reactions to frustration, an experiment was set up in a clothing factory with three matched experimental groups by Coch and French (1955). There was no participation by workers in the control group in planning the production changes to be made although the reasons and the nature of the changes were explained to them. A second group was represented in the planning activities through their elected representatives. The third group participated personally in designing the changes to be made. The author concluded from this study that the non-participation procedure had the effect of causing members of the group to identify the management as hostile to their interests.

It is possible for an extension worker to modify greatly or remove completely any group resistance to changes decided upon in planning the programme. This change can be accomplished by the use of group meetings in which the need for change is effectively communicated and by group participation in planning changes. In an experiment Morrow (1957) demonstrated that the county organisation could be involved in every step of programming. Compared with the procedure previously followed in the experimental block, the improved procedure resulted in involving 489 more families, 898 more individuals, 23 more planning meetings and participation by 21 more townships than had participated in the past.

Limitations of organised participation

The participation approach has its limitations. It was found to be more effective in the situation described above. However, it does not justify some of the extravagant claims that have been made for it in industrial management situations. It needs considerable skill to use the method successfully. Participative leadership does not eliminate disagreement, which can be strong in a participative setting as under non-participative conditions. However, disagreements can be aired and coped with in a constructive manner.

The extent of members' expectation and readiness to accept participative leadership methods also determine their effectiveness. The degree of participation that is most effective may depend on the history of the organisation. All organisations use 'participation' to some degree, although with some it may be limited merely to informing people of decisions and being willing to listen to objections to them.

Wilkening (1958) found that a substantial proportion, about one-third, of the agents reported that the organisation should be involved during or after the programme is planned but not before. This view is obviously contrary to the principles and philosophy developed in the preceding studies.

Effect of organised participation of people on the value of decisions

Most of the research shows that group solutions to problems that were arrived at with opportunities for discussion and exercise of pressure within the group are more correct than they would have been without this opportunity (Thorndike, 1938). In group discussion, the right solutions tend to win out. The more frequent correct solutions to problems by groups as compared to solutions by individuals can be attributed to the high frequency of rejection of incorrect suggestions by the group (Shaw, 1932). Generally the observed superior performance of groups in problem-solving was found to reflect the performance of the most capable member (Marquart, 1955).

The atmosphere in an organised participative approach may be 'permissive or autocratic'. If a permissive atmosphere prevails, it may ensure that every suggestion is heard and receives consideration. Under an autocratic procedure, the group may discourage the presentation of unusual ideas and quickly reject one offered by an individual. Important decisions which affect many people, are not likely to be left to individuals but participation by those who will be affected increases understanding and commitment to the goals and to the methods of attaining them. Therefore, it may be concluded that group problem-solving is more efficient in the long run than reaching decisions solely by expert thought and advice (Marquart, 1957 and Shaw, 1932).

Barnard (1946) stated that organisational decisions that represent a concensus of opinion are usually logical because they have been formulated, at least to some degree.

Form and structure of county programme-planning committees

The research studies conducted by Gwinn (1958), Beckstrand (1959), Lacy (1961), O'Connell (1961), Voorhees (1960) and Blackburn (1964) reported that the lack of an overall design for the structure and functions of programme-planning groups was causing confusion among those involved in the planning process.

Beach (1961) found that the largest number of respondents (committee members) of his study tended to favour 25 members as the desirable size for a committee. They also favoured a 2 to 1 ratio between men and women members.

Qualifications and selection of planning committee members

Trecker and Harleigh (1954) in their book Committee Common Sense made the following statements regarding the qualifications of a good chairman:

i) To be effective, a chairman must be able to preside at meetings and lead discussion. The manner in which the chairman presides is important in creating a climate that (a) encourages participation, (b) allows all ideas or contributions to be heard, (c) keeps the general and specific purposes of the session before the group and (d) contributes to determining and attaining the organisation's objectives.
ii) Familiarity with the purpose of extension education and the function of the committee.
iii) Action-oriented in possessing the drive for accomplishment

in and as a result of the session of the organisation.

iv) Willing to study and learn the business of the committee and effective procedure for the chairman's job.

Tippots (1960) found that the extension agents used the following ways to secure memberships of the general committee: (i) appointed by an official body (29.8%), (ii) chosen by the extension staff (28.7%), (iii) selected by an unofficial group (12.8%) and combination (28.7%). He found that the most frequently used method of becoming a member of a special committee was by appointment by the general committee (47%). However, all his respondents considered a combination of methods for selection for special committee members either 'very good' or 'good'.

Beach (1961) found that his respondents (36 committee members) collectively considered the 'ability of a person' the major basis for selection but that the upper aged group favoured 'ability of a person' more while the lower aged group favoured 'representatives of business'.

Studies conducted by Jahns (1961), Heard (1962), O'Connell (1961) and Voorhees (1960) revealed that the extent and quality of involvement in the programme-planning process was related to their possession of certain personal and social characteristics by the committee members.

Farrell (1964) reported that influential persons were more aware of the problems of the community and were more likely to view themselves as being able to resolve the problems.

Training methods for organised participants

Sanders (1962) found that those who have been trained through discussions at meetings are most active on committees but those who received training in several different ways proved more active than those who received their training from a single source.

Characteristics Associated with Members, Perception, Participation and Performance

Wilkening (1958) in a study of role definitions found that very few members of the block extension programme planning committee voluntarily indicated that a major objective of their work was accomplishing sectional, state or national objectives.

Generally the block agricultural committee tended to reinforce the local orientation of extension work. The study showed that members of the Wisconsin County Agricultural Committee tended to hold a more traditional view of extension work than did county extension agents. This same trend was present in other states, especially those in which emphasis had recently been given to making substantial adjustments to changed conditions in agriculture and living in rural areas. Wilkening (1958) suggested that more educational work needed to be done with the organisations in many states and counties to achieve consensus regarding the changed roles of agents and the new elements in the roles of the organisations and their members.

Sarbaugh (1960) in a study of Noble County in Ohio (USA) found that only a few respondents (out of 164) knew how the county extension programme was developed; most did not know the duties of the extension advisory councils. They did not participate in selecting council members and, as a consequence, passed on the opportunity to express personal preferences regarding the extension programme through council members. The most frequent forms of contacts with county extension agents were through visits and correspondence. Respondents tended to participate and to assume leadership in non-extension rather than extension organisations. Subject-matter content and the opportunities for sociability were the main reasons given for attendance at extension meetings; lack of interest or time, transportation problems, health and not being invited were the major reasons for non-attendance. Women participated more and in a wider variety of areas than did men.

O'Connell (1961) identified that committee members in the older aged group (41–54) participated in extension programme planning more than younger members. Similarly, college educated members participated more than high school graduates. Committee members who had been more extensively involved in extension activities participated more and so did those who had a favourable attitude towards extension. Differences in occupation, involvement in other organisations and knowledge of extension did not affect their participation.

Sanders (1962) found that committee members tended to be younger, better educated, of a higher socioeconomic level and more male dominated. Among his several comparisons of participation levels, he noted a positive relationship with socio-economic status, organisational experience, training in and knowledge of the rural development programmes and satisfaction with both the programme and agency personnel, access to mass communication media and proximity of residence to centres of population concentration. He found that male members under 40 or 50 years of age, those who had attended college and the self-employed were more apt to be among the more active participators.

Heard (1962) found a positive correlation between the performance in the committee situation and age, education and membership in other organisations. He found no particular relationship between performance and either previous extension participation or attitude towards extension.

Conclusion

Douglas (1968) reviewed the programme-planning research conducted at the University of Wisconsin and drew the following conclusions:

i) Training the professional extension educators who are to provide leadership for planning until they thoroughly understand the objectives, policies and procedures of the planning process, can significantly contribute to the effectiveness of the planning effort.
ii) Getting local people of a community, especially those in the power structure, to realise the need for and to accept the concept of planning through a planned process of social change, increases the effectiveness of the planning effort.
iii) The development of an overall design for the structuring and functioning of a planning group facilitates the process of planning.
iv) The degree of contribution of local people to the planning is related to their possession of certain personal and social characteristics.
v) The effectiveness of the planning effort depends to a considerable extent on the orientation and training of those who are to be involved in the planning process.
vi) The use of background information by planning groups

presents one of the more serious difficulties encountered in the total programme-planning process.

Concerns for Future Research

Some of the major concerns and problems in programme planning that warrant research are listed below.

General framework

1. What principles should be kept in view while formulating an extension programme?
2. What conditions or criteria should be fulfilled in order to ensure that the conditions of a particular principle have been met?
3. What is the most effective and effective model for planning a programme? How should each stage in the model be operationalised?
4. What kinds of policies need to be identified with respect to the programme function?
5. What should be the roles of administrators, supervisors, specialists and extension workers in programme planning?
6. What are the most effective methods of training extension personnel to do programme development?

Organisation for planning

7. What should be the specific roles of the programme-planning committee?
8. What criteria should be used to ensure a good representative and effective programme-planning committee?
9. What are the most effective methods of training programme-planning committee members for their roles and responsibilities?
10. To what extent is the existing organisation for planning extension programmes sound and effective?

SITUATION ANALYSIS

11. What are the various 'decision-making' theories and what implications do they have for the extension programme-planning process?
12. What type and kind of background information is essential for programme planning?

13. What should be the roles of specialists, extension workers and Panchayat Samiti members in collecting and assembling background information in planning programmes?
14. How can real problems be identified?

Stating objectives

15. What are the most effective methods of stating objectives?

Selecting problems

16. What are or should be the criteria for establishing priorities?

Finding solutions

17. To what extent should Panchayat Samiti members be involved in thinking through possible solutions to the problems that have been identified?

Programme action

18. How are plans effectively translated into action?
19. When and how should adjustments, if needed, be made in the planned programme?
20. How can the annual plan of work be used to facilitate co-ordination of staff efforts with respect to major programme concerns?

Evaluation of results

21. How can evaluation be built into the total programming process?
22. What are the most effective methods of evaluating planning procedures and programme accomplishments?
23. How can the programme accomplishments be reported to the public and relevant groups?

12

A Critical Look at Extension Programme Planning

Extension programme planning is a decision-making, social action process in which extension educationists involve people's representatives to determine their needs, problems, resources and priorities in order to decide on an extension programme consisting of the situation, problems, objectives and solutions that will form the basis of extension teaching plans for a given period. Extension programme planning is a positive, dynamic, useful and effective term only when the concepts involved are understood and applied. However, this concept is being attacked from all aspects. There is confusion about its nomenclature, its purpose and the validity of its principles and procedures. Hence a critical look at the various aspects of this process is needed.

Proper Nomenclature

The process followed for planning extension programmes has been given many names—extension programme planning, building, development, determination, area planning etc. In extension literature, the terms extension programme planning, building and determination are used synonymously and interchangeably. However, Matthews (1962) makes a distinction between extension programme planning and programme development and says that the latter refers to total extension programme planning and implementation operation.

Programme projection is an expanded concept of extension

programme planning and grew out of the discussion which took place in the 1955 session of the Extension Committee on Organization and Policy (ECOP). Programme projection is long-range planning and is broader in scope. It is a more complete and more balanced approach. The term area planning, first used in 1956, refers to developing programmes for the people of underdeveloped rural areas. However, an expansion and reorganisation of area-planning took place in 1961 and the programme was redesignated as the rural area development programme.

On the basis of the above discussion, it may be argued that the most widely accepted term to designate the process through which extension programmes are developed is extension programme planning. Other terms, such as programme projection, programme determination etc., are used for special purposes.

Is it a Process?

Almost all the definitions of extension programme planning imply that it is a process. However, Bruce (1964) remarked that 'we have no evidence at all indicating that there is such a thing as a planning process'. He further stated that some extension workers had for years carried out highly successful programmes without engaging in formal programme planning. He went on to show that the conventional methods of programme planning do not always provide an efficient basis for devising working programmes, particularly in new subject-matter areas and with a new audience. However, Matthews (1962) had suggested that extension programme planning is a process that does not naturally have a definite form and structure. While many authors have described this process as a series of steps, Matthews (1962) viewed it as a continuous cycle.

It seems Bruce (1964) had something different in mind about the concept of process than is generally held in the literature. A process is 'any phenomenon which shows a continuous change in time', or 'any continuous operation or treatment'. 'If we accept this concept of process, we view events and relationships as dynamic, ongoing-ever-changing, continuous'. As Berlo (1966) stated: 'When we label something as a process, we also mean that it does not have a beginning, an end, or a fixed sequence of events'. Viewed from this angle, we can say that there is not yet any conclusive evidence about the nature of the planning process. But the researches conducted by Kincaid (1964), Beal et al. (1966) do suggest that extension programme planning can be viewed as a process of a series of events or things to be accomplished.

Purpose of Programme Planning

Some people are critical of the time spent by extension workers in programme planning. One should only be critical of time spent in planning if the resultant plans are useless, ineffective or inadequate in making efficient and effective use of the time and talent of the extension workers and people. If at any time a plan is not useful in the action programme, the criticism must rest on the planners or those guiding the planning process, not on the concept of planning. Planning properly done is an investment of time that should pay high dividends.

The first consideration for anyone who is concerned with a process or a set of procedures for planning is to clearly identify the primary purpose of the planning process to be developed. Many have suggested that the purpose of planning is to educate those who participate. However, Vandeberg (1967) pointed out that the primary purpose of any planning, first and foremost, is that of developing a sound, defensible and progressive extension programme. In the process followed, many other benefits might accrue, such as the education of participants. But the primary purpose is to develop an extension programme which can and will be implemented. In developing such a programme we should not waste the time of those participating in planning. We should take support from any source that offers help in planning a good extension programme and not for educating those involved.

Validity of Principles and Procedures

According to Bruce (1964), probably no other single professional activity of the extension worker receives as much time and attention as does programme building. This concept has been a topic of seminars, courses, workshops, training, meetings, circular letters and individual correspondence. Yet there the distinct possibility exists that our procedures for planning and the principles on which they are based are inadequate for our purposes and in many cases, just plain wrong. Bruce (1964) supported this contention with two kinds of evidence.

First is the fact that some recalcitrant extension workers have for years carried out highly successful programmes without engaging in formal programme planning at all. It is impossible to say how many more have merely gone through the motions of programme planning to meet a formal requirement. In spite of this, the activities of many of these workers are forward looking, purposeful and obviously constitute an organised effort.

Secondly, the old procedures and concept of programme planning do not always provide an efficient basis for devising workable programmes for new areas of subject matter and new audiences.

Conventional methods of programme planning are often inefficient. The general practice of beginning the planning procedures with a general description of the situation often results in the collection of useless information.

Conventional procedures offer little or no guidance for converting the objectives and situational data into workable teaching activities. The result is that an extension worker, even after describing the situation on the basis of an adequate analysis, has difficulty in using the results of the planning activity in any meaningful manner to arrive at specific teaching methods.

The conventional procedures are also preoccupied with objectives. While the focus on objectives is desirable, it is also necessary to consider realistically the problem of implementing programmes to achieve them. Observation would indicate that the availability of resources does affect what we try to do, at least to the point of affecting our choice among acceptable objectives. From a practical point of view, a planning procedure which does not provide for determining resource needs, for testing the availability of resources and for resource allocation, cannot guide us as to the feasibility of the plan it produces and hence is incomplete.

Conventional procedures for programme planning are usually stated in terms of things to be done rather than things to be accomplished. We are told, for example, not only that the situation must be explored (a thing to be accomplished), but that we must use a committee of lay leaders to explore it (a thing to be done). No allowance is made for possible differences in situations or in people or in the kind of planning involved.

We seem to assume that piling up masses of situational data will somehow give rise to objectives and thus to teaching activities. It is logically impossible to make any systematic observation of a situation in the absence of some objective. Every position in an extension organisation has certain objectives built into it, deriving from the purpose for which the organisation was established. Failure to recognise these general objectives as limits in programme development can lead to the collection of useless data and the development of unacceptable plans.

We also tend to assume that all good planning will follow a single process which always begins with a problem and ends with a solution. In fact, this is true only part of the time. Much of our planning in extension is concerned with finding objectives to be reached by already selected methods. What else is it when we plan how best to use a block fair or a regularly scheduled radio programme for educational purposes which have not yet been determined? Is it reasonable to expect that a set of procedures designed to work in an 'objective-to-method' situation will work in a 'method-in-search-of-an-objective' one?

It is much easier to point out the supposed shortcomings of our programme building process than to propose workable remedies. One reason our current practice works poorly at certain tasks is that the tasks are difficult to perform. Bruce (1964) has suggested the following ways of looking at programme planning to solve some of the difficulties listed above:

1. We must accept planning as a continuing way of solving educational problems, rather than a series of specific activities undertaken at certain times of the year and resulting in a written programme. Some ways of analysing and solving problems may well be better than others, at least for certain purposes. But planning, as a problem-solving technique, should apply at levels of problems, from the written five-year plan to the strategy for the next ten minutes of a discussion.

2. We must be careful to think of the process(es) of programme planning as a series of events or things to be accomplished rather than a series of specific activities or proce-

dures. We can think of understanding the situation as one event in the process, for example, knowing that it may be accomplished in some cases by a survey committee and in other cases by an extension worker from his own knowledge. If we are going to use organised planning at all levels of problems, we have to keep our methods flexible.

3. We must be alert to the possibility that different situations may call not just for different planning procedures, but for entirely different planning processes. For example, the planning for a single show in a television series begins with the general teaching methods already chosen. (It is unlikely that you would decide to substitute a meeting at the last minute.) This process may be entirely different from that used in planning a resource development programme wherein even the more specific objectives have not been reasoned out but even the most general methods have not been chosen. Procedures which would produce a good plan in the one instance might be useless in the other. We should be flexible enough to do both kinds of planning well.

4. We must be efficient in the use of our time and that of others. If we narrow our objectives from the general to the specific before trying to describe the situation, we can secure more specific data. We would thus get only what we need for a given bit of planning and avoid the accumulation of useless bits of detailed information. We must also avoid involving people in planning when their involvement would serve no real purpose.

5. We must deal realistically with the problems of implementation. We cannot in the end do more than we are equipped to do. Considering problems of securing and allocating resources at all stages of planning would permit us to adjust our expectations to what is possible.

6. We must take a more objective view of the involvement of lay people in programme planning. Their involvement in some programme planning tasks at certain levels might be an efficient means of programme building. For example, they often have information necessary in planning not otherwise available to us. We may also involve lay people in programme building for reasons other than the efficient production of workable plans. We may involve them as a means of teaching them to plan, or because we believe in the right of the responsible adult to take part in planning things which affect him. We may hold the theory

that involving our clients in planning will secure their support in carrying out the programme. These are all good reasons but none of them has any functional relation to planning. It is important that we recognise this involvement as a means to an end and use it only when the results justify it.

Conclusion

An attempt has been made to point out some areas in which our present planning methods may be out of tune with present needs and to suggest some ways of improving them. No specific procedures have been suggested because procedures will vary with the situation, the kind of problem and the person doing the planning. There has been another reason as well: we do not know enough about the nature of planning to make specific recommendations.

If we are to find out more about programme planning in extension, there is something for each of us to do. All of us, especially extension workers and specialists, can become more conscious of our planning techniques and can study and experiment in an effort to become more proficient in this area. Administrators and supervisors can assist in this through direct help and guidance and ensuring that planning requirements and procedures are flexible enough to permit experimentation. Standard procedures are often the fossils of obsolete methods. The teachers and researchers in this and related fields can contribute by increasing our understanding of planning itself. This means studying its various applications, as in industry or national defence, and from the point of view of other disciples. Most importantly, however, it means doing empirical research on the nature of programming rather than studying the procedures associated with it or attempting to construct procedures built on incomplete knowledge. We must have more solid fact and less assumptions.

Appendix I

Principles of Extension Programme Planning

The principles of extension programme planning as stated by various authors are presented below:

I. **Fanning (1928)**

1. Agricultural program development is a way of doing extension work.
2. Agricultural program development is the coordinated responsibility of the county agent and the home demonstration agent.
3. Agricultural program development is the basis for the extension plan of work.
4. Representative farm leaders are the primary participants in agricultural program development.
5. Agricultural program development is cooperative with all agencies and groups, public, civic and otherwise concerned with the welfare of the farm people.
6. Agricultural program development is thoroughly democratic in all its procedures.
7. We as agricultural extension workers believe in its fundamental importance and soundness in bringing about better living among and for rural people.

II. **Brunner (1944)**

1. Democratic method has been successful and should be encouraged. By participation the program becomes their's (the people's).

2. Democratic education is helped by use of locai, unpaid volunteer leaders.
3. Whenever and wherever possible, extension activities should be related to existing agencies such as cooperatives, churches, schools etc.
4. Extension is for all classes, although groups and classes within communities, do exist in many societies.
5. A community approach in many parts of the world may involve a wider extension program than we have in the United States.
6. Extension personnel must recognize that one of their chief functions, as leaders, is to help people to become aware of the needs both immediate and long time.
7. Extension process facilitates change and helps people adjust to changes forced from outside by new inventions, markets and political developments.
8. Extension education aims at actions, but on a community level extension can well assist in organizing for desirable action, though it does not of itself take that action.
9. Extension program must be based on conditions that exists be they local, regional, national and international.
10. All-round programs must be developed gradually. People must be led not pushed-allowed to understand and gain confidence.
11. A well-balanced program can and should be as broad as the recognized needs of rural life.
12. Program must be flexible, changing as needs and conditions change.
13. Extension should not deal simply with men but also women, boys and girls.
14. Extension program must be correlated and harmonized with national policy.

III. Knans (1948)

1. Program planning is a continuous process.
2. Program planning is a teaching process.
3. Established definite objectives is an essential part of the planning process.
4. Good program will be based on and grow out of basic information, recognized problems and felt needs of local people.

5. Proper program planning procedures lead people to see beyond personal felt needs to basic underlying problems.
6. Good program planning develops leadership.
7. A well-planned program will contain procedures for evaluation.
8. The function of the extension staff in program planning is to provide democratic leadership.

IV. Jans (1952)

1. Is based on the needs of the people.
2. Is comprehensive in scope.
3. Is flexible.
4. Is an educational process.
5. Starts where people are.
6. Requires capable local leadership and makes use ot technical and research information.
7. Seeks maximum local participation in efforts to help people help themselves.

V. Kelsey and Hearne (1949)

Sound extension program building:

1. Is based on analysis of the facts in the situation.
2. Selects problems based on needs.
3. Determines objectives and solutions which offer satisfaction.
4. Has permanence with flexibility.
5. Has balance with emphasis.
6. Is a continuous process.
7. Is a coordinating process.
8. Is a teaching process.
9. Has a definite plan of work.
10. Provides for evaluation of results.

VI. Matthews (1952)

1. Program development is a continuous process engineered by the extension worker.
2. In program development, the roles performed by those who have a part are very important. However, the roles of the extension agent and the lay person are very different.
3. Program development is an educational process.
4. Extension programs are based on recognized problems and needs of the local people.
5. Extension programs grow out of the local social and economic situation.

6. Decisions about what the program shall be are reached cooperatively by extension agents and the people.
7. Definite procedures are followed in developing a program.
8. Sound program planning procedures, coordinate the efforts of many individuals, groups, organizations and agencies.
9. Program development requires considerable time from members of the planning bodies, extension agents and other active participants.
10. Program is written for recording and communicating to all interested and concerned, what is expected to be accomplished and the general means to be used.
11. A sound program is practical in terms of objectives, available leadership, extension staff and other needed resources.
12. A written annual plan of work is an aid in implementing the program.
13. The program and annual plan of work provide for and facilitate evaluation of results.

VII. Maunder (1956)

1. Program planning should be based on a careful analysis of factual situation.
2. Program should be oriented to the existing technical, economic and social level of the rural people of the area.
3. Program should be comprehensive, including activities of interest to all social and economic groups.
4. It should be educational and be directed towards bringing about improvement in the ability of people to solve their own problems, individually and collectively.
5. Extension program should be arrived at democratically through the participation of lay people, entire extension staff and others who can contribute.
6. Organization should be used as a tool to accomplish objectives.
7. Maximum use of voluntary leadership should be made in the planning as well as in the execution of extension programs.
8. Program should be flexible to meet long-time situations, short-time changes and special emergencies.
9. Select problems for action which will meet recognized needs.

10. Objectives should be clearly defined at all levels in terms that people will understand.
11. Good program planning provides for evaluation of results.
12. Extension program should be carried on by well-trained personnel, effectively supervised.
13. Program should be achievable considering such factors as personnel, finance, time and facilities.

VIII. Holman (1957)

1. Sound program building is based on an analysis of the facts of the situation.
2. Sound program building selects problems based on needs.
3. Good program building determines objectives and solutions which offer satisfaction to the village farmer or his family.
4. Good program has permanence with flexibility.
5. Good program must be comprehensive enough to embrace the interest and needs of all age groups, creeds and races.
6. Good program has a definite plan of work.

IX. Raudabaugh (1957)

Sound program development:

1. Is a teaching and learning process.
2. Is a continuous process which provides for continuity as well as flexibility.
3. Is planned with and not for the people.
4. Is based on and grows out of recognized problems and felt needs of local people.
5. Is based on an anlysis of facts, local, state, national and international.
6. Includes cooperatively determined objectives which offer satisfaction.
7. Includes a definite plan of work.
8. Provides for evaluation to show results in terms of changes in the action of people.

X. Rassi (1960)

1. Program planning is a continuous process considering permanence and necessary flexibility.
2. Program planning is an excellent teaching and leader-training process.
3. Establishing definite objectives is an essential part of the program planning activities.

4. Program building is that process which gives guidance and direction.
5. Good program will be based on and grow out of basic information, recognized problems and felt needs of local people.
6. Good program has to have balance with emphasis.
7. Objectives at all levels are to be measurable and attainable.
8. Well-developed program is necessary to give direction to the annual plan of work and a prerequisite to effective teaching.
9. Well-developed extension program is to be understood by the extension staff and local people.
10. Well-planned program will contain procedures for evaluation.
11. The function of the extension staff in program planning is to provide democratic leadership.
12. Proper program-planning procedures lead people to see beyond present felt needs to basic underlying problems and unfelt needs.

XI. Leagens (1961)

1. Effective rural development programs must have clear and significant objectives.
2. To achieve the broad purposes of community development requires planning at the top level and also at lower levels including the states, districts, blocks and villages.
3. There are no unplanned programs.
4. The most effective rural development programs result when there is general agreement among village, block, district, state and national officials on three important items:
   i) a basic philosophy regarding program development;
   ii) a clear policy that reflects the basic philosophy; and
   iii) a workable procedure that gives general direction but provides ample latitude for adjustments needed to meet local situations.
5. Programs are most effective when based on adequate and current facts pertaining to local conditions as well as those related to national and rational situations.
6. Selection of a relatively small number of the most significant needs singled out for major attention contributes to the effectiveness of rural development programs.

7. Skillful involvement of progressive village leaders is fundamental in planning rural development programs.
8. Programs that are planned for longer periods of time than one or two years tend toward greater effectiveness.
9. Procedures in rural programing that fairly assure integration of problems related to the farm, the home and the community appear to contribute to their soundness and effectiveness.
10. Program planning must take into account cultural values and the social system.
11. Program content must be determined with care and preciseness.
12. Interpretation of the program to officials and nonofficials and to the general public is an essential step in successful programming.

XII. USDA (1962)

1. Involve people in planning the extension education program.
2. Make the extension program family-based, including agriculture and home economics for youth and adults.
3. Begin with a limited number of extension activities.
4. Start with some phases of each area of extension program.
5. Use the methods found effective in the early days of U.S. extension development.
6. Employ meetings to teach groups, as soon as possible, in the development of a new program.
7. Employ teaching aids which are not beyond audience's comprehension.
8. Develop leaders to actually teach and carry on other functions in the educational program.
9. Start working in very limited number of pilot areas to develop and demonstrate an extension program.
10. Don't expect too much too soon. Changes that last come slowly.
11. Remember that the rural people are not unintelligent just because they are illiterate.
12. Begin with needs which people recognize and want to satisfy.
13. Consider the different social patterns in a community.
14. Determine what factors cause people of other cultures to change.

XIII. Vidyarthi (1961)

1. Describe the particular situation, then base the program on it.
2. Select problems and fix priorities based on felt needs.
3. Objectives and goals should offer satisfaction.
4. Good programs have permanence with flexibility.
5. Good programs combine balance with emphasis.
6. Prepare a plan of work.
7. Programing is a continuous process.
8. Programing is an educational process.
9. Programing is a coordinating process.
10. Program planning provides for evaluation of results.

XIV. Singh (1962)

1. A sound programme must focus on the needs of farmers.
2. Sound programme planning should start with the people where they are.
3. It must have a definite plan of work no matter how well the programme is thought through.
4. Good programme building should determine clearly stated objectives and solutions which offer satisfaction.
5. A good programme should have a balance with items of assistance for all major social, economic and age groups.
6. It must focus on problems that are 'most important' since it cannot be 'all things to all people' at the same time.
7. It must provide for a system of priorities in line with local needs, interests and resources.
8. It must provide satisfaction for the people who participate.
9. A good programme should provide for evaluation of results.

Appendix II

Extension Programme Planning Models

Various models of extension programme planning available in extension education literature are given below:

Warner (1955) suggested the following steps for programme planning:

1. Analysis of local situations
2. Determining objectives
3. Plan of action
4. Calendar of work
5. Evaluation of results

Maunder (1956) was one of the pioneers to propose a definite working model of the extension programme-planning process:

1. Collection and analysis of data
2. Determination of needs and objectives
3. Defining problems
4. Finding solutions
5. Selecting problems and determining priorities
6. Preparing a plan of work
7. Carrying out the plan
8. Checking and evaluating results
9. Review of progress and projections of plan

Raudabaugh (1957) suggested five stages for planning extension programmes:

1. Identification of the problem
2. Determination of the objectives
3. Development of a plan of work

4. Follow through on the plan of work established
5. Determination of progress

According to USDA (1959), the following programme-planning procedure should be followed:

1. Situation analysis
2. Organization for planning
3. Program planning process
4. The planned program
5. Plan of work
6. Execution of plan of work
7. Appraisal of accomplishment

Matthews (1962) developed a Program Development Cycle Model with the following steps:

1. Organization for involving people
2. Planning process
3. The planned program
4. Annual plan of work
5. Teaching and related activities
6. Evaluation and reporting

Chang (1963) proposed a triangular model for extension programme planning with the following steps:

1. Programme Determination
   —Describe
   —Analyse
   —Identify problem
   —Consider alternatives
   —Formulate objectives
2. Programme Implementation
   —Decide goals
   —Decide subject matter to be taught
   —Decide teaching methods to be used
   —Fix responsibilities
   —Work out a calendar of work
   —Prepare lesson plans
   —Evaluate plans
3. Results
   —Find out degree of success
   —Discover new problems

Rudramoorthy (1964) suggested a model with the following steps:

1. Assess the situation
2. Identify problems
3. Define objectives
4. Find solution
5. Fix priorities
6. Draw up a plan of action
7. Put the plan to action
8. Evaluate results
9. Review progress

Boyle (1965) after an extensive review of the literature, developed a programme-planning process consisting of the following five phases:

1. Formulation of a broad organizational philosophy, objectives, policies and procedures for program planning in the state.
2. Identification and clarification of a need and preparation for planning country programmes.
3. Organization and maintenance of country planning groups.
4. Reaching decisions on the problems, concerns and opportunities.
5. Preparation of a written program document.

According to Bradfield (1966), Extension Programme Planning consists of the following steps:

1. Collect facts
2. Analyze facts
3. Define problem
4. Propose solutions
5. Plan work
6. Develop program
7. Evaluate
8. Reconsider situation and plan next programme

Dahama (1966) suggested that the following steps considered in extension programme planning.

1. Study the situation
2. Identify the local leaders and obtain their support
3. Set up a planning committee
4. Determine important needs and interests of the people
5. Set up objectives
6. Fix priorities
7. Decide teaching objectives and teaching methods

8. Periodically review the situation and reconsider the plan

Peason (1966) identified eight steps in the programme-planning process:

1. Collect facts	Program Planning
2. Analyze situation	
3. Identify problems	
4. Decide on objectives	
5. Develop plan of work	Program Action
6. Execute plan	
7. Determine progress	
8. Reconsideration with evaluation at each step	

Kahn (1969) suggested a model with anchor points in planning:

1. Planning instigators
2. Explorations
3. Defining the planning talk
4. Policy formulation
5. Programing
6. Evaluation and feedback

Singh (1970) listed the following steps for Extension Programme Planning:

1. Collect facts
2. Analyse situation
3. Identify problems
4. Decide on objectives
5. Develop plan of work
6. Execute plan
7. Determine progress

Brereton (1972) listed five steps for developing an extension programme:

1. Need determination
2. Setting programme objectives
3. Programme design
4. Programme implementation
5. Programme evaluation

According to Green and Winstead (1975), systematic planning should include the following steps:

1. Identification and evaluation of problems and opportunities
2. Clarification and evaluation of mission, goals and objectives
3. Determination of priorities
4. Analysis and evaluation of capabilities

5. Development and execution of program of action
6. Identification and monitoring of future developments that will have a major impact on program of results
7. Allocation of essential resources
8. Acceptance and support of key people who are involve or affected.

References

Aiken, Charles. 1958. Identification of Procedures Associated with Teaching Effectiveness of New York County Extension Agents. Ph.D. Thesis, Cornell Univ., Ithaca, N. Y.

Allen, H.B. 1953. *Rural Reconstruction in Action.* Cornell Univ. Press, Ithaca, N. Y.

Barnard, H.W. 1946. *Psychology of Learning.* McGraw Hill, Inc., N. Y.

Beach, R. 1961. The Organization and Operation of a Long Range Programme Planning Committee. M. (eds.) Sc. Thesis. Purdue Univ., safayette, Ind.

Beaglehold, Severyn. 1955. *Human Perspective in Sociology.* Prentice Hall, Inc., Englewood Cliffs, N.J.

Beal, G.M., J.M. Bohlen and J.N. Raudabaugh (eds.). 1965. *Leadership and Dynamic Group Action.* Iowa State Univ. Press, Ames, Iowa.

Beal, G.M. et al. 1966. *Social Action and Interaction in Planning Process.* Iowa State Univ. Press, Ames,

Beavers, I. 1962. Iowa County Agents. *Perception of Programme Planning.* University of Wisconsin Ph.D. Thesis, Univ., Madison, Wisconsin.

Beckstrand, G.L. 1959. *Organizational and Operational Procedures of Extension Advisory Councils.* University of Wisconsin Ph.D. Thesis, Univ., Madison Wisconsin.

Bennett, C.F. 1977. Analyzing *Impact of Extension Programmes.* Washington D.C. U.S.D.A.

Berlo, David. K. 1960. *The Process of Communication.* New York: Holt, Rinehart and Winston Inc.

Bhatnagar, O.P. 1987. *Evaluation Methodology for Training.* Oxford & IBH, Publ. Co., New Delhi.

Bible, R. et al. 1960. The role of executive committee in the county extension organization in Pennsylvania. Penn. State

Univ., Park, Pa.

Biddle, W.W. 1953. *The Cultivation of Community Leaders.* Harper & Brothers, Inc., N. Y.

Bilokury, Omar G. 1958. A concept of programme planning in agricultural extension. M.S. Seminar Report. Univ. of Wisconsin, Madison, Wisc.

Blackburn, D.J. 1964. An Appraisal of Various Aspects of the Extension Programme in Columbia County. M.Sc. Thesis. Univ. of Wisconsin, Madison, Wisc.

Bliss, R.K. 1952. *Spirit and Philosophy of Extension Work.* Washington: USDA.

Bloom, B.S. (Ed.) 1960. *Taxonomy of Educational Objectives.* New York: David Mckay, Inc.

Boone, Edgar J. (ed.). 1962. *A Research Approach to Programme Development in Cooperative Extension.* National Agri. Extension Centre for Advance Studies, Madison, Wisconsin.

Boone, Edgar J. 1985. *Developing Programs in Adult Education.* Eaglewood, Cliff. N.J. Prentice-Hall

Boyle, Patrick C. and Johns, Kans. 1970. in *A Research Approach to Program Development in Cooperation Extension.* Madison, Wisconsin: National Centre for Advance Studies.

Boyle, Patrick C. 1965. *The Programme Planning Process with Emphasis on Extension.* NAECAS, Madison, Wisconsin.

Boyle, Patrick C. 1958. An Analysis of Selected Programme Planning Principles. Ph.D. Thesis. Univ. of Wisconsin, Madison, Wisc.

Bradfield, D.J. 1966. *Guide to Extension Training.* FAO, Rome.

Brar, B.S. 1966. Contribution of Sarpanches in Planning and Execution of Agricultural Extension Programmes, Ludhiana. M.Sc. Thesis. PAU, Ludhiana.

Brereton, P.R. 1972. Developing extension programs. *Journal Coop. Extension*, vol. X, no. 1.

Bruce, R.L. 1964. *A look at programme planning. Journal Coop. Extension*, vol. II, no. 2.

Brunner, Edmes S. de. 1944. Conference Report on the Contribution of Extension Methods. USDA, Wash., D.C.

Brunner, E.S. de, E.N. Sanders and D. Ensminger (eds.). 1947. *Farmers of the World.* Columbia. Univ. Press, N. Y.

Brunner, E.S. de and Yang C. 1949. *Rural America and the*

Extension Service. Columbia Univ. Press, N. Y.

Bryson, Lyman. 1936. *Adult Education*. American Book Co., N. Y.

Carter, Cecil E. 1964. The Relattion of Leaser Behaviour Dimensions and Group Characteristics of County Extension Advisory Committee Performance. M.SC. Thesis. Ohio State Univ., Columbus, Ohio.

Cernea, M.M. and Tepping, B.J. 1977. *A System of Monitoring and Evaluating Agricultural Extension Projects*. Washington, D.C. The World Bank.

Chang, L. 1963. in *Cooperative Extension Work*. New York, Comstock Publ. Co.

Clark, H.F 1960. An Analysis of the Training Needs of Wisconsin County Service Personnel. Ph.D. Thesis. Univ. of Wisconsin, Madison, Wisc.

Coch, Lester and J.R.P. French. 1955. *Readings in Social Psychology*. Holt, Rinehart & Winston, Inc., N.Y.

Dahama, O.P. 1966. *Extension and Rural Welfare*. Ram Prasad & Sons, Aigra.

Dickon, A. and K. Doston 1961. *Principles and Concepts in Program Planning*. Univ. of Tennessee, Knoxville Tenn.

Dickon, A. and K. Doston, K. 1961. *The Tennessee County Agricultural Extension Program Development Handbook*. Univ. of Tennessee, Knoxville, Tenn.

Douglas, Mohd. A. 1968. Programmeplanning research. *Journal Coop. Extension*, Vol. VI, No. 1.

Edwards, Milton. 1962. A Study of Mississippi County Agents' Percepta of Rural Areas Development. M.Sc. Thesis. Univ. of Wisconsin, Madison, Wisc.

Ensminger, Douglas. 1954. *A Guide to Community Development*. Ministry of C.D, Govt. of India, New Delhi.

Fanning, J.W. 1928. County Long-time Farm and Home Program. Atlanta, Georgia. State Cooperative Extension Service.

Farmer, L. 1959. A Study of the Collection and Use of Factual Information by Tennessee Extension Agents. Univ. of Tennessee, Knoxville, Tenn.

Farnsworth, W.F. 1963. A Study of County Extension Agents Program Planning Role. Ph.D. Thesis. Univ. of Wisconsin, Madison, Wisc.

Farrell, G.M. 1964. Influential Persons' Awareness of Community

Problems in Rural Wisconsin County. M.Sc. Thesis. Univ. of Wisconsin, Madison, Wisc.

Franco, Joseph di. 1958. A Collection of Principles and Guides. Comparative Extension Pub. No. 4. Cornell Univ., Ithaca, N.Y.

Frutchery, Fred P. 1956. Principles of Extension Teaching. Cir. no. 242. USDA, Wash., D.C. Govt. of India. Planning Commission. 1957.

Govt. of India. 1961. *Extension Education in Community Development.* Ministry of Food & Agric., New Delhi.

Govt. of Punjab. 1961. *Block Development Plan—Its Preparation and Extension.* C.D. & P. Deptt., Chandigarh.

Guame, J.W. 1963. A study of Difficulties Expressed in Programme Planning. M.Sc. Thesis. Univ. of Wisconsin, Madison, Wisc.

Gwinn, S.M. 1958. The Role of County Advisory Committees in Programme Projections. Ph.D. Thesis. Univ. of Wisconsin, Madison, Wisc.

Green, L. and Winstead, R. 1975. in a Collections of Principles and Guides. Comparative Ext. Pub. No. 4. Cornell Uni., Ithica. N.Y.

Hammonds, Cursie. 1950. *Teaching Agriculture.* McGraw Hill Book Co., N.Y.

Heard, R.F 1962. An Analysis of Problem Identification Process in Oconto County. M.Sc. Thesis. Univ. of Wisconsin, Madison, Wisc.

Hill, William. 1959. A Status Study of Program Development in Ten Southern States. Ph.D. Thesis. Univ. of Wisconsin, Madison, Wisc.

Holhubner, F.J. 1962. A Study of Illinois County Extension Council Members' Understanding of Their Responsibilities. M.Sc. Thesis. Univ. of Wisconsin, Madison, Wisc.

Hollan, Lines B. 1965. *Helping Committees Achieve Objectives and Maintain Interests and Satisfaction.* USDA, Washington, D.C.

Holman, Wendill. 1957. Principles of programme planning. USAID, New Delhi. (mimeographed).

Houle, A.W. 1961. In: *Leadership and Dynamic Group Action.* G.M. Beal et al. (eds.) Iowa State Univ. Press, Ames, Iowa.

Isaacson, C.L. 1960. Principles and Procedures for Developing County Extension Programmes. M.S. Thesis. Univ. of Arizona,

Tucson, Ariz.
Jahada, A. and R. Barnit. 1955. *Educational Measurement.* American Council on Education, Washington D.C.
Jahns, Irwin R. 1961. A Method of Evaluating Performance of Members in Programme Pianning Group. M.Sc. Thesis, Univ. of Wisconsin, Madison, Wisc.
Jans, F.C. 1952. Extension Looks at Programme Planning. Cir. no. 478. USDA, Washington D.C.
John, Provinse. 1960. Community development and evaluation. *Community Development Review*, vol. 12.
Kallander, G.F. 1961. *Establishing a Home Science Extension Program.* Coop. Extension Pub. no. 4, Cornell Univ., Ithaca, N.Y.
Kapanigowda, Ankegowda. 1961. A Review of Selected Principles and Procedures Useful in the Planning of County Agricultural Extension Programmes in the United States with Application to C.D Programme Planning in India. M.Sc. Thesis. Univ. of Tennessee, Knoxville, Tenn.
Kelsey, L.D. and C.C. Hearne 1949. *Cooperative Extension Work. Ithaca.* Comstock Publ. Co., New Delhi.
Kincaid, James M. (Jr.). 1962. A Suggested Model for Evaluating the Cooperative Extension Programme Planning Process. M.Sc. Thesis. Univ. of Wisc., Madison, Wisc.
Kincaid, James M. (Jr.). 1964. Minnesota Extension Workers' Evaluation of a Proposed Set of Cooperative Extension Program Planning Concepts. Ph.D. Thesis. Univ. of Wisconsin, Madison, Wisc.
Klinberg, O. 1955. *In: Social Research and Social Policy.* H.E. Freeman and C.C. Sherwood (eds.). Prentice-Hall, Inc., Englewood Cliffs, N.J.
Kahn, Karl. 1969. Note-book in program development Ext. summer-session. Madison, Univ. of Wisconsin. (Memographed).
Knans, Karl. 1948. Note-Book in Program Development. Extension Summer Session. Univ. of Wisconsin, Madison, Wisc.
Koontz, H. and C.O.'Donnell. 1959. *Principles of Management.* MCGraw Hill Book Co., Inc., N.Y.
Lacy, M.P. 1961. The Effects on Involvement on the Participation in Extension Program Planning in Wanpaca County. Ph.D. Thesis. Univ. of Wisconsin, Madison, Wisc.
Lawernce, Roger L. 1962. *The Program Planning Development*

Manual. Iowa State Univ., Ames, Iowa.

Leagans, J. Paul. 1946. *Extension Evaluation—Extension Objectives.* USDA, Washington D.C.

Leagans, J. Paul. 1961. Extension Programme Building. In: *Extension Education in Community Development.* Ministry of Food & Agric., New Delhi.

Marquart, Dorothy. 1955. Group problem solving. *Journal Social Psychology,* vol. 4, no. 3

Matthews, J.L. 1952. National Inventory of Extension Methods of Program Determination. Cir. no. 447, USDA, Washington D.C.

Matthews, J.L. 1956. Program planning views. *Extension Service Review,* vol. XXV, no. 3.

Matthews, J.L. 1962. What is program planning all about. *Extension Service Review,* vol. XXXI, no. 2.

Maunder, A.H. 1956. In: *Methods and Program Planning in Rural Extension.* J.M.A. Penders. H. Veenman and Zenen, Wageningen, the Netherlands.

Mayer, Alert. 1958. *Pilot Project India.* Univ. of California Press, Berkeley, Cal.

McCormick, R.W. 1959. An Analysis of Training Needs of Extension Agents in Ohio. Ph.D. Thesis. Univ. of Wisconsin, Madison, Wisc.

McCormick, R.W. 1963. Guiding principles that apply in developing the functions and organization of committees. *Programme Development Workshop for County Extension Agents. The OSU, Columbus, Ohio.*

Mehta, R.C. 1966. A study of the farmers' involvement in farm planning in the IADP District, Pali, Rajasthan. *Indian Journal Extension Education.* vol. 1, no. 4.

Mohammad, Shah. 1960. NESA Regional Extension Seminar. Report. Ministry of food & Agric, New Delhi.

Molner, August. 1989. *Community Forestry—Rapid Appraisal.* FAO, Rome.

Morris, F.B. 1937. *Planning County Agricultural Extension Programs.* Cir. no. 260. USDA, Washington D.C.

Morris, M.P. 1961. The Effects of Involvement on the Participation in Extension Program Planning in Wanpaca County. Ph.D. Thesis. Univ. of Wisc., Maidson, Wisc.

Morrow, E.R. 1957. Long-range Integrated Programming for

Adult Education. Ph.D. Thesis. Univ. of Chicago, Chicago, Ill.

Musgraw, B.E. 1962. *Organization and Operating Agricultural County Councils,* Michigan, Illinois: Coop. Extension Service.

Myerson, M. and Edward Banfield. 1935. *Politics, Planning and the Public Interest. The Case of Public Housing in Chicago.* The Free Press, Glenoe, Illinois.

Nieder, Frank. 1960. Programme Projection. USDA, AEP 176, Washington D.C.

Nieder, Frank. 1956. County Extension Organization and Related Social Factors. Cir. no. 448. USDA, Washington D.C.

Norby, Oscar W. 1961. An Appraisal of Long-time Cooperative Extension Program Planning in Wanpaca County. Ph.D. Thesis. Univ. of Wisconsin, Madison, Wisc.

O'Connell, T.E. 1961. A Study of the Decision Makers of a Program Planning Subcommittee. M.Sc. Thesis. Univ. of Wisconsin, Madison, Wisc.

Olson, Kenneth S. 1962. *What Research Tells Us about Building An Extension Program—A Program Aid.* Univ. of Arizona, Tucson, Ariz.

Peason, Lynn L. 1966. *Extension Program Planning with Participation of Clientele: The Cooperative Extension Service.* Prentice-Hall, Inc., Englewood Cliffs, N.Y.

Penders, J.M.A. 1956. *Methods and Programme Planning in Rural Extension.* H. Veenman and Zenen, Wageningen, The Netherlands.

Perkins, C. 1970. Analysis of goals in complex organizations *American Sociological Review,* vol. 35, no. 1.

Govt. of India Planning Commission. 1957. Report of the Team for Study of Community Projects and National Extension Service. vol. I. New Delhi.

Price, Randel K. 1960. An Analysis of Educational Needs of Arkansas Extension Agents. Ph.D. Thesis. Univ. of Wisconsin, Madison, Wisc.

Rao, G. Rama. 1964. Principles in Programme Planning Extension. Ministry of Food & Agric., New Delhi.

Rassi, Jaffar. 1960. NESA Regional Extension Seminar Ministry of Food & Agri., New Delhi.

Raudabaugh, J. Neil. 1957. Essentials of Sound Extension Program, ER & T-277 (12-57). USDA, Washington D.C. (mimeographed).

Reid, Y. and A. Wilson. 1933. In: *Leadership and Dynamic Group Action* J.M. Beal et al. (eds.) Iowa State Univ. Press, Ames, Iowa.

Roland, M. 1961. In: *Leadership and Dynamic Group Action* J.M. Beal et al. (eds.) Iowa State Univ. Press, Ames, Iowa.

Ross, M.G. 1967. *Community Organization—Theory, Principles and Practice.* Harper & Row Publishers, New York.

Rowen, L.A. 1965. In: *Evaluation Research.* Edwards A. Suchman (ed.) Russell Sage Foundations, N.Y.

Rudramoorthy, B. 1964. *Extension in Planned Social Change.* Asia Pub. House, New Delhi.

Sabrosky, R. 1966. A critique of community services. *American Journal Public Health*, vol. 56, no. 3.

Sanders, E.N. 1962. Participation of Rural Development Committee in Sharp County. M.Sc. Thesis. Univ. of Arkansas, Fayetteville, Ark.

Sandhu, A.S. 1965. An Appraisal of the Procedures Followed in Planning Agricultural Extension Programme at the Block Level in Punjab. M.Sc. Thesis. PAU, Ludhiana.

Sandhu, A.S. 1970. Procedures followed by village level workers for conducting agricultural method demonstrations. *Indian Journal Extension Education*, vol. VI, Nos. 1 & 2.

Sandhu, A.S. 1993. *A Textbook of Agricultural Communication: Process and Methods.* Oxford & IBH Publishers, New Delhi.

Sandhu, A.S. and T.S. Sohal, 1965. An appraisal of the knowledge of block extension staff about extension programme planning. *Indian Journal Extension Education*, vol. 1, no. 3.

Sandhu, A.S. and T.S. Sohal 1966. Involvement of Panchayat Samiti members in planning agricultural extension programmes. *Extension in Asia*, vol. V, no. 2.

Sandhu, A.S. and T.S. Sohal 1966. Procedures followed in planning agricultural extension programme at the Block level in Punjab. *Indian Journal Extension Education*, vol. II, Nos. 1 & 2.

Sandhu, A.S and T.S. Sohal 1966. Planning agricultural extension programme at the block level. *Indian Journal Extension Education*, vol. II, nos. 3 & 4.

Sarbaugh, M.M. 1960. Factors Related to People's Knowledge and Participation in Extension Programs. M.Sc. Thesis. Univ. of Wisconsin, Madison, Wisc.

Sears, Jesse B. 1950. *The Nature of the Administrative Process.* McGraw Hill Book Co., New York.

Seepersad J. & Henderson, T.N. 1984. Evaluating Extension Programmes in *Agricultural Extension. A Reference Manual.* Rome. F.A.O.

Settlemyer, R. 1958. Some methodological problems of field studies. *American Journal Sociology*, vol. 72, no. 2.

Sharma, L.D. 1968. A Study of the Role of Agricultural Extension Officers in Programme Planning at the Block Level in Punjab. Ph.D. Thesis. PAU, Ludhiana.

Shaw, K.E. 1932. A comparison of individual and small groups in relation to solution of complex problems. *American Journal Psychology*, vol. XV, no. 4.

Singh, M.R. 1966. A study of farm production plans under intensive agricultural district programme. *Indian Journal Extension Education*, vol. II, nos. 3 & 4.

Singh, Rameshwar B. 1962. Report on the NESA Regional Extension Seminar. Ministry of Food & Agric., New Delhi.

Singh, K.N. 1970. In: *Research in Extension Education.* New Delhi, Indian Society of Ext. Edu.

Solem, James and H.D. Werner. 1968. PPBS: A Management Innovation. *Journal Cooperative Extension*, vol. VI, no. 4.

Sprowls, F.J. 1959. A Study of Organized Extension Programs in Oregon and Washington. M.Sc. Thesis. Univ. of Wisconsin, Madison, Wisc.

Stauber, R.L. 1968. PPBS for extension. *Journal Cooperative Extension*, vol. VI, no. 4.

Steele, J.D. 1970. *Organization in Action.* McGraw Hill Book Co., New York.

Stogdill, Ralph M. 1959. *Individual Behaviour and Group Achievement.* Oxford Univ. Press, New York.

Straughn, A.A. 1963. A Study of the Perceived Role of County Extension Agents in Program Planning. Ph.D. Thesis. Univ. of Wisconsin, Madison, Wisc.

Stufflebeam, D.L. (ed.). 1971. *Educational Evaluation and Decision Making.* Itasca, Ill. Ithica: NY: Cooperative Extension Service.

Sutton, W.H. 1961. Extension in a changing society *Extension Service Review*, vol. 32, no. 3.

Taylor, Carl C. 1956. *A Critical Analysis of India's Community*

Development Programme. Govt. of India, Ministry of C.D. New Delhi.

Taylor, D.B. 1976. Alternative Evaluation Models *North Central Association Quarterly* vol. 50. pp. 353–358.

Thelan, H.A. 1958. *The Dynamics of Groups at Work*. Univ. of Chicago Press, Chicago. Ill.

Thiband, R. and P. Helley. 1959. *The Social Psychology of Groups*. John Wiley & Sons, N.Y.

Thiede, R.L. 1964. *Measurement in Education*. John Wiley & Sons, N.Y.

Thompson, Merrit M. 1943. The levels of objectives in education. *Harvard Educational Review*, no. 13.

Thorndike, R.L. 1938. The effects of discussion on the correctness of group decisions when the factor of majority influence is allowed. *Journal Rural Sociology*, vol. 9, no. 3.

Tippots, D.H. 1960. Continuity of Programme Projection in a County Extension Programme. M.Ed. Report. Ohio State University, Columbus, Ohio.

Trecker, R. and A. Harleigh. 1954. *Committee Common Sense*. William Morrow & Co., Inc., N.Y.

Tyler, Ralph W. 1950. *Basic Principles of Curriculum and Instruction*. Univ. of Chicago Press, Chicago, Ill.

USAID. 1962. *Extension Development Around the World—Guidelines for Building Extension Organizations and Programs*. USDA Washington D.C.

USDA. 1956. *Program Development Process* HQ-ER & T-348. USDA, Washington D.C.

USDA. 1956. *Findings from Research on Meetings*. USDA, Washington D.C.

USDA. 1957. Essentials of Sound Extension Program Development. ER & T-277. USDA, Washington D.C.

USDA. 1959. *Guidelines for County Extension Program Planning and Projection*. ER & T-83. USDA, Washington D.C

Vail, Q.S. 1953. Developing a County Agricultural Extension Programme. M.Sc. Thesis. Univ. of Mississippi, University, Miss.

Vanderberg, Gale L. 1965. Getting the most from planning councils. *Extension Service Review*, vol. XXX, no. 3.

Vandeberg, Gale L. 1967. Guidelines to planning. *Journal Coop. Extension*, vol. V, no. 3.

Vidyarthi, G.S. 1961. Developing family, village and block programmes, In: *Extension Education in Community Development*. Govt. of India, New Delhi.

Villalbos, Fiol, B. 1962. A Study of Difficulties Experienced by Extension Personnel in Programme Development. M.Sc. Thesis. Univ. of Wisconsin, Madison, Wisc.

Voorhees, Wilbur. 1960. A Study of Characteristics and Contributions of Programme Planning Committee Members. M.Sc. Thesis. Univ. of Wisconsin, Madison, Wisc.

Wallace, E.H. 1963. A Study of New Mexico County Agents: Perception of Rural Areas Development. M.Sc. Thesis. Univ. of Wisconsin, Madison, Wisc.

Washington Conference. 1955. Guidelines for Building Extension Organization and Programs. USDA. Washington D.C.

Warner, K.F. 1955. Extension Program Planning Washington D.C. USDA. (Memographed Notes)

Whiteman, D.C. 1952. Background Information Needed for Planning County Agricultural Extension Programs. M.Ed. Thesis. Colorado State College, Mreelay, Colo.

Wilkening, Eugene A. 1958. Consensus of role definitions of county extension agents between the agents and local sponsoring committee members. *Rural Sociology*, vol. 23, no. 2.

Williams, C.G. 1959. An Analysis of Selected Principles Related to Programme Planning Process. M.Sc. Thesis. Univ. of Wisconsin, Madison, Wisc.

Subject Index